# The SECRET PATH

A western interpretation of
Ramana Maharishi's teachings.
Before you pass from your body
all these Truths will become
evident. There are many
treasures here for you.

Love Dave

Dr. Paul Brunton

# The
# SECRET PATH

## A Modern Technique for Self-Discovery

## Dr. Paul Brunton

SAMUEL WEISER, INC.
York Beach, Maine

# CONTENTS

CHAPTER                                                 PAGE

I. WITH A WISE MAN OF THE EAST . . . 11

II. MAN—SCIENCE'S GREATEST RIDDLE! . . 22

III. THE MYSTERIOUS OVERSELF . . . . . 34

IV. THE PRACTICE OF MENTAL QUIET . . . 45

V. A TECHNIQUE OF SELF-ANALYSIS . . . 56

VI. A BREATHING EXERCISE TO CONTROL
THOUGHTS . . . . . . . . . . 69

VII. THE AWAKENING TO INTUITION . . . . 75

VIII. THE AWAKENING TO THE OVERSELF . . 91

IX. THE WAY OF DIVINE BEAUTY . . . . 104

X. THE GOSPEL OF INSPIRED ACTION . . . 109

XI. SPIRITUAL HELP IN MATERIAL AFFAIRS . 116

XII. THE EPILOGUE . . . . . . . . . 125

*The works of Dr Brunton*

In chronological order

A SEARCH IN SECRET INDIA

THE SECRET PATH

A SEARCH IN SECRET EGYPT

A MESSAGE FROM ARUNACHALA

A HERMIT IN THE HIMALAYAS

THE QUEST OF THE OVERSELF

DISCOVER YOURSELF

INDIAN PHILOSOPHY AND MODERN CULTURE

THE HIDDEN TEACHING BEYOND YOGA

THE WISDOM OF THE OVERSELF

THE SPIRITUAL CRISIS OF MAN

# A PERSONAL NOTE

Dr. Paul Brunton died July 27, 1981, in Vevey, Switzerland. Born in London in 1898, he authored thirteen books from "A Search in Secret India" published in 1935 to "The Spiritual Crisis of Man" in 1952. Dr. Brunton is generally recognized as having introduced yoga and meditation to the West, and for presenting their philosophical background in non-technical language.

His mode of writing was to jot down paragraphs as inspiration occurred. Often these were penned on the backs of envelopes or along margins of newspapers as he strolled amid the flower gardens bordering Lac Leman. They later were typed and classified by subject. He then would edit and meld these paragraphs into a coherent narrative.

Paul Brunton had lived in Switzerland for twenty years. He liked the mild climate and majestic mountain scenery. Visitors and correspondence came from all over the world. He played an important role in the lives of many.

"P.B.", as he is known to his followers, was a gentle man. An aura of kindliness emanated from him. His scholarly learning was forged in the crucible of life. His spirituality shone forth like a beacon. But he discouraged attempts to form a cult around him: "You must find your own P.B. within yourselves," he used to say.

KTH

# FOREWORD

TO-DAY an interesting change has come over Western thought. We can discuss the fact of the soul without being considered either unduly religious or mildly unbalanced. We affirm or deny the existence of the self as freely as we discuss the atom or the sources of history. This is a significant step forward and indicates a growing sensitivity to that "mysterious Overself" referred to by our author.

Modern psychologists can be broadly divided into those who affirm the presence of a controlling integrating self within the body-nature, and those who affirm only the existence of the mechanical form. Is there a self? Is there a subjective reality? Is there such a thing as spiritual consciousness? This is the problem before investigators to-day in the field of human awareness. Can the hidden self be proved and people be induced to tread the secret path to the holy place, where the self can be discovered?

The timeliness of this book is real. It expresses, with a beautiful clarity, truths which have been too often hidden under ponderous phrase, difficult Oriental symbolism, and mystical vaguenesses. It will be welcomed by those who are alive to the moment's urgency and to humanity's new readiness for spiritual revelation. Man's deeply realised need has prepared him to tread the Secret Path.

Humanity stands to-day at the gate of reality. Man is learning to recognize, and desire, the world of spiritual being. He is rapidly apprehending the significance of that deeper being which is hidden behind the mask of the personality. To find that deeper being, to reveal its nature, and to function consciously in the world of truth in which it dwells—this is man's immediate task and for this the years of modern distress have prepared him.

That the "Kingdom of God is within" is the message of the Ages, and thousands are now seeking the Hidden Way that leads to that Kingdom. Arrived there, we find the sources of all inspiration: we discover the point where the intellect is transmuted into the intuition: we enter the realm of illumination. The reward given to those who enter the citadel of the soul is TRANSFIGURATION,—the radiance which pours through a rapidly changing personality.

In that secret place we join the ranks of the Great Intuitives, the inspired Companions of God. We find ourselves amongst those who must save the world, for that has ever been God's way of salvation. The appeal to-day is for those who know, who have seen and who have understood. Understanding, they will welcome the message of this book and feed its progress. It carries the flame of inspiration, and will lead to that inspired action, practical spirituality, and dedicated service, which is the hall-mark of the revealed Soul. Is anything more deeply needed to-day?

ALICE A. BAILEY,
Author of *From Intellect to Intuition.*

# CHAPTER I

SOME years ago I wandered for awhile through sun-baked Oriental lands, intent on discovering the last remnants of that "mystic East" about which most of us often hear, but which few of us ever find. During those journeyings I met an unusual man who quickly earned my profound respect and received my humble veneration. For although he belonged by tradition to the class of Wise Men of the East, a class which has largely disappeared from the modern world, he avoided all record of his existence and disdained all efforts to give him publicity.

Time rushes onward like a roaring stream, bearing the human race with it and drowning our deepest thoughts in its noise. Yet this sage sat apart, quietly ensconced upon the grassy bank, and watched the gigantic spectacle with a calm Buddha-like smile. The world wants its great men to measure their lives by its puny foot-rule. But no rule has yet been devised which will take their full height, for such men, if they are really worth the name, derive their greatness not from themselves but from another source. And that source stretches far away into the Infinite. Hidden here and there in stray corners of Asia and Africa, a few seers have preserved the traditions of an ancient wisdom. They live like ghosts as they guard their treasure. They dwell outwardly apart, this spectre-race, keeping alive the divine secrets which life and fate have conspired to confide in their care.

The hour of our first meeting is still graven on my memory. I met him unexpectedly. He made no attempt at formal introduction. For an instant, those sybilline eyes gazed into mine, but all the stained earth of my past and the white flowers that had begun to spring up on it, were alike seen during that one tinkle of the bell of time. There in that

11

seated being was a great impersonal force that read the
scales of my life with better sight than I could ever hope
to do. I had slept in the scented bed of Aphrodite, and he
knew it; I had also lured the gnomes of thought to mine
for strange enchanted gold in the depths of my spirit: he
knew that too. I felt, too, that if I could follow him into
his mysterious places of thought, all my miseries would
drop away, my resentments turn to toleration, and I would
understand life, not merely grumble at it! He interested
me much, despite the fact that his wisdom was not of a
kind which is easily apparent and despite the strong reserve
which encircled him. He broke his habitual silence only
to answer questions upon such recondite topics as the
nature of man's soul, the mystery of God, the strange powers
which lie unused in the human mind, and so on, but when
he did venture to speak I used to sit enthralled as I listened
to his soft voice under a burning tropic sun or pale crescent
moon. For authority was vested in that calm voice and inspiration gleamed in those luminous eyes. Each phrase that
fell from his lips seemed to contain some precious fragment
of essential truth. The theologians of a stuffier century taught
the doctrine of man's original sin; but this Adept taught the
doctrine of man's original goodness.

In the presence of this sage one felt security and inward
peace. The spiritual radiations which emanated from him
were all-penetrating. I learnt to recognize in his person
the sublime truths which he taught, while I was no less
hushed into reverence by his incredibly sainted atmosphere.
He possessed a deific personality which defies description.
I might have taken shorthand notes of the discourses of
this sage; I might even print the record of his speech; but
the most important part of his utterances, the subtle and
silent flavour of spirituality which emanated from him, can
never be reported. If, therefore, I burn literary incense before his bust, it is but a mere fraction of the tribute I
ought to pay him.

One could not forget that wonderful pregnant smile of
his, with its hint of wisdom and peace won from suffering
and experience. He was the most understanding man I have
ever known; you could be sure always of some words from
him that would smooth your way a little, and that word always verified what your deepest feeling told you already.

And yet, in its settled moments, his face bore an expression of deep melancholy; still it was a resigned melancholy, not the bitter rebellious kind one often sees. . . . You knew that at some period of his past he had suffered some inexpressible agony.

The words of this sage still flame out in my memory like beacon lights. "I pluck golden fruit from rare meetings with wise men," wrote transatlantic Emerson in his diary, and it is certain that I plucked whole basketfuls during my talks with this man. Our best philosophers of Europe could not hold a candle to him. But the inevitable hour of parting came. Time turned around this old globe of ours, I went back to Europe, busied myself with one thing and another, and quite lately prepared to return to the East once more. I purposed no less a thing than an exploration right across Asia, an exploration that would continue my old quest of the last surviving exponents of genuine Oriental wisdom and magic. I hoped to wander through the yellow deserts of Egypt and among the wisest sheikhs of Syria; to mingle with the vanishing fakirs of remote Iraq villages; to question the old Sufi mystics of Persia in mosques with graceful bulbous domes and tapering minarets; to witness the marvels performed by Yogi magicians under the purple shadows of Indian temples; to confer with the wonder-working lamas of Nepal and the Tibetan border; to sit in the Buddhistic monasteries of Burma and Ceylon, and to engage in silent telepathic conversation with century-old yellow sages in the Chinese hinterland and the Gobi desert.

My kit was almost packed, my last few papers were being put in order, and I was nearly ready to leave. I turned my face away from the crowded streets of the great city in which I lived.

"London is a roost for every bird," wrote shrewd Disraeli, and I must be one who is somewhat old-fashioned. I like the quiet London of eighteenth-century streets and dignified old railed-in squares and I regard them as welcome oases in a prevailing desert of noisy modernity. I see the satin-coated and knee-breeched ghosts of a past century when I walk around the pleasant grassy squares at night. I dislike the London which provides a stage for countless motors and hurrying people. I am fond of the London which hovers around the wide Thames at places like Rotherhithe and Wapping, for there, among the picturesque old wharves and barnacled quays, I stroll in an atmosphere faintly

redolent of the sea and I watch romantic-looking craft
come and go on the river. I prefer to see a weather-beaten
barge take its tranquil way a'down the Thames to a painted
demon of a lorry pursuing its nerve-racking, noisy route
along the street.

And so this fateful day I sought a few hours' escape
among certain friendly trees in the green country-side. I
found them after traversing rolling chalk hills, winding
lanes and quiet beech woods. My eyes became half-closed,
the harsh confused noises of thronged towns had faded,
and I was once more sitting in almost tranced stillness. It
was not long before old habit reasserted itself and I expectantly drew out a worn note-book. I sat down in the
lush green grass with pen in hand and book upon the
knee, seeking to cast my net upon the delicate thoughts
and beautiful moods which swim across the heart when all
is still. It is in such solitary rural silence that I have often
felt more at ease than in many a city drawing-room, and
it is when companioned by such silvery beeches that I have
often felt a more beautiful and sincere presence than with
many human beings.

It was the mellow autumn season, and all around me
were the gold and green tinted leaves which lie down to
die in such profusion when the life of the year begins to
fail. The late afternoon sun shone generously upon everything around. The hours slipped past one another, the soft
murmur of a few insects rose and died away as they flew
through the air, but still the pen lay motionless between
my fingers. One waits beside the silent shore of the mind
for the coming of exalted moods whose fragile bodies are
as gossamer. So soft are they that if one does not cast
one's net aright, the rough cords of mortal tongue will slay
the tiny wanderers with brutal touch, and so shy are they
that one must sometimes wait long before the first timorous
alien will venture into the net. But once a few captives
have been gathered together, the reward descends rich
upon one's heart.

In this spiritual element lie all the fragrant hopes of
man, waiting, like so many unplucked flowers, for the soft
hands which shall garner them for a sightless people. These
visitations of a loftier mood provide one with jewels for
one's writings. In such sacred moments one touches the
infinite. Sentences form themselves from the ether, one

hardly knows how; phrases disengage themselves from the skies and descend upon this sublunary world to feed one's pen. One must yield to these mysterious moods, and not resist them. Thus does one render oneself worthy to become a mediator between the immortal gods and frail forgetful man.

To-day, however, I thought that I had waited in vain and so closed the book and replaced the pen in my pocket. Soon the strange hour of twilight would shade the face of time and then the soft feet of night would creep into the halls of day. Thereafter, I would rise up from the fallen trunk where I had moodily pondered in vain, and with slow steps I would stumble homewards over the darkened fields and through woods which over-ripe leaves had carpeted a rich brown.

But instead there came a strange pause, and a film fell across my eyes making the sense of sight oblivious of the earth-world around me. The ichor leapt in my veins, flinging the sluggish blood aside, while a great yellow light seemed to shine within my heart. A hand seemed to touch my shoulder, so I raised my head and looked upwards, to find a benignant face bent over me.

And he whom I had known in the Orient, the Wise One of the East, appeared before me, his grave bearded face as clear, as recognizable as though it were there in the flesh. Certainly he came to me with a tread which was as silent as the fall of fresh dew. I made the humble obeisance of my heart in veneration and greeting. His strange eyes turned remonstratingly upon me.

He said gently: "*My son, it is not well. Hast thou forgotten compassion? Shalt thou go forth to add to thy store of knowledge while others starve for the crumbs of wisdom? Wilt thou commune with the Divine Ones when there are those who look for God but perceive only the impassable barrier of the sky: when there are those who throw their prayers to a void which returns no answer? Stay thy feet if needs be but forget not thy fellows in distress. Leave not for the lands of waving palms until thou hast well regarded these words. May peace be ever with thee!*"

And, thereupon, without another word, he passed out of my vision, as silently and as mysteriously as he had appeared.

§

When I became aware of my environment, I could barely
see the trees again for it was grown dark; the light had
faded out of the day, and the scintillating stars were coming
to birth in the sky. The first wan rays of the moon threw
a few gleams upon the fallen tree. I could see little else.

I arose and made the homeward journey. As I walked
through the grass, with stick trembling in my hand and
with thoughts fastened upon the august utterance which
had fallen from those reproving lips, I suddenly realized
that the accusation was perfectly true. I had considered
none save myself. I had followed the light of the star of
Truth, the star which attracted me most out of the whole
sky, but I had followed it for myself alone.

I left my country-side musings and returned to town, entering with a strange awe its streets so canopied by the
darkness of night. Here were millions of beings compelled
by the demands of society to go to bed at the behest of
a clock and to rise at the ringing of a noisy alarm bell.

Yes, I had supped alone, feasting on divine verities that
can never die. Would not my own soul grow lean and small
if I disdained those who were hungry for that which I had
taken freely out of the seemingly impenetrable silence of
the sky?

Could one rest with the mere recovery of these truths
for oneself? There are other people in this populous world,
and among them a few who might welcome such thoughts
as I could give them.

The world of fact has little sympathy with the man who
stands aloof and keeps his soul free for visions in which
it does not share. And the world is right. We who are
seers and mystics have to draw the last crystal drop of
water from out the well of vision, but with that begins our
duty, stern and strict, of offering the unfamiliar drink to
the first wayfarer thirsty enough to accept it. Not for ourselves alone, but for all alike does Neptune cast his magic
trident over the deep places of the soul and show us his
glamorous pictures therein.

If the privilege of sitting at the feet of forgotten but
none the less potent gods is indeed high, then the travail
of carrying their message to an unheeding yet suffering
people is just as high, just as noble. Perhaps no man's mind

is so clothed in ugliness that a few faint gleams of hidden
beauty do not trouble him now and again and cause him
to raise his head a little towards the stars, sometimes in
perplexity at the meaning of it all, sometimes in wonder
at the ceaseless harmony of the spheres.

*"Forget not thy fellows in distress,"* my strange visitant
had told me.

What then could I do? I could not tarry overmuch in this
Western country and neglect my trans-Asiatic expedition,
for which the pressure of fate and the pull of inclination
had conspired to smooth my path. How then, for the sake
of one's fellows, could one assume the prophetic mantle
and hat and go out to spread what one had learnt to regard as truth?

And the answer rose up clearly in my mind in the shape
of a self-evident thought. I would set down some of the
things which life had taught me and then leave the written
record behind. I could but call at the doors of men and
deliver a few thoughts which had helped me, and then I
must withdraw and leave the latter to do their mission.
I could not undertake to play the advocate on their be-
half; whoever would receive them readily should surely be
helped, too, but whoever rejected them might find elsewhere his meat and drink. Could my record but meet with
a man at some crucial troubled moment of his life, who
knew how far it might guide him towards the Eternal Good?
I would try to put into the words of that book a wisdom
learnt from dearly-bought experience. There would be sentences that would hold the marrow of days spent in mourn-
ing, and phrases would fall from my pen which would
embalm tears that once fell from my eyes. I would do all
this because I should like those pages to carry healing
and consolation to those who are in present distress, to
show them that man contains rare and unexpected resources
within himself, wherewith to meet and overcome the hard
trials which few can escape. But it need not, therefore,
be a joyless book. For it would also hold the lingering
echoes of many happy hours spent in sublime peace; it
would more than hint at the ecstatic enjoyment of diviner
states which are open to man. No, it need not be a joyless
book, indeed it could not be. The flowers must drop their
petals, one by one, the moon waxes and must wane, even
the lark's fine song must one day be stilled; but I have

found a Land where strange flowers grow, and grow for ever; where the sky's light is never less; and where all things sing an immortal music that has not ceased since time began.

Thus the pages which follow took their genesis. If they seem to consist of little more than a collection of scattered thoughts loosely tied together, I must ask the pardon and indulgence of the reader. For I gather my written thoughts in the motley; they are always disjointed and come only in fragments. I stand ashamed before the facile orations of other men, whose sequences flow like a stream of oil. This halting utterance of mine I attribute to a natural impulse of my mind to enter into a state of rest, rather than to enter into a state of activity. There is a war in my heaven every time I take up my pen, which has accepted the limitations with which it was born and does not aspire towards a better technique.

It will be observed that there is very little argument in these pages, but very much that will provoke it. The reason will be plain to those who have mastered the mystery of Christ's saying, "Except ye become as little children ye shall not enter the kingdom of heaven," but it will be hard to grasp by the ultra-clever, the super-shrewd and the ego-centred. For intellect is but a machine; it makes a splendid servant yet a bad master.

We are apt to criticize where we do not comprehend. Where something here indited appears difficult to grasp or seems superficially obscure, the reader should neverthe-less ponder upon it until he reaches the point of discovery.

If I can stimulate him to discover his own true thought, I render him better service than if I teach him. This age reads in order to kill time; but a few wise ones read in order to make time alive. I hope the latter will find this book.

Crusading holds no charms for me and agitating would be but a torment. Rather would I be a stimulator, stimulating others not to join some cult, but to think for themselves, and to think deeper than the conventional men of our time.

It is only by thinking a matter out for oneself that we understand it best. I cannot hope to convey my understanding to you, but I can hope to arouse that faculty within you which will give you perception. Hence these writings do not formulate any fixed system, which you have to swallow by an act of faith. They aim at being suggestive. They try to challenge you to think for yourself. They provide you with mental nuts to crack in the form of unusual questions. You can create a new system of ideas for yourself by musing upon these pages, but it will be your own system, not another's. Such thoughts as these may begin by startling you, but they may end by stimulating you, I do not know.

I am not writing for the benefit of the man who has already put up the shutters of his mind and firmly fixed them, in case the light of a few new ideas might stream in and disturb his sleep. I am writing for the few who amid the modern muddle of bewildering doctrines have placed their feet upon tentative ground because there seems no safer place in sight.

§

Those who look for plenty of facts in this book will not find them; there are thousands of books which will give them all the facts they can ever want; and better still there is the voluminous Book of Life which they can always consult and in which they can always verify every statement I have made. My aim has been to give the soul of all these facts; I have tried to sum up in one flash of a sentence what lies *behind* a hundred thousand facts, events and experiences.

Because I spent the years stretching my philosophic soul upon the rack until I found the truth, I am in no mood to listen to polished platitudes nor to write them. Yet really there is nothing new in the essential thought behind these pages, though it does not matter so much whether these are new or whether they are neglected thoughts, as whether they are TRUE thoughts. Medieval men like Thomas à Kempis and Jacob Boehme communicated the same thought in earlier centuries, but they communicated it in a form which makes no great appeal to me and will make even far less appeal to my contemporaries. Yet they wrote out of a veridic experience which any man of the twentieth century may duplicate, if he will. Those who regard this experience as inconceivable at most and illogical at least, should investigate before they snatch at such final conclusions. For I know that I have tried to tackle this difficult investigation of Life in a scientific yet reverent spirit, to approach it with an impartial love of Truth for its own sake and not in order to confirm or refute any particular theories. That I should treat seriously of little-known states of consciousness in this book may seem superstition to the many, but it is true Science to me. Those who can receive it in this light will find their faith rewarded by time, who will likewise pay their credulity with first-hand knowledge.

My confidence stands serene and unshaken that I can make good my thesis against all comers, but only if they are prepared to undertake the same psychological experiments which I undertook. The thoughts I now give out did not come to me after long argument; they came after long experience. Whoever, therefore, would understand them aright, must be willing to invite the same experience, and this will come readily enough if he is as keen on finding truth as he is on his other and more mundane affairs.

If, therefore, I find the spiritual life no less substantial than the material one, so can every reader of this book. I possess no especial privilege which other human beings do not possess; I can claim no magic gift which has not been fought for by continued effort. What I have found within myself is precisely what anyone else, even a hardened Chicago gangster, may find in his own self too.

If the phrases of this book are occasionally fervent and sometimes heated, this can be explained only because it is a transcript from life; not a collection of academical theories evolved amid the quiet cloisters of a Cambridge. Can no one be a good philosopher unless he writes coldly, as though he took no interest in his subject? Must his pages be pale and colourless, must he carefully prune all emotional expressions out of them, before he is safe reading?

The critic cannot refute this work because it is based, not upon my human intellectual opinions, but upon eternal truths as old as the starry heavens that greet our gaze at night, truths that are imbedded in both Nature and man. They are there, but they must be dug out.

This book is but one voice crying in the wilderness of this stricken world; there are others and in many countries. The message it carries in its pages is simple yet subtle.

It is a literary arrow drawn and disposed at a venture, but it is yet guided by a higher hand than mine. Fate, the needs of many persons who have written to me, and the expressed wish of this Wise Man of the East, one of my spiritual Guides, have all conspired to thrust this work upon me. The book will find its way into the expectant hands of some men and women who care for Truth and it may serve them.

§

I have endeavoured to give faithful report to a Voice which appears to be dumb in most men; therefore I hope these printings will be not without some value to them. The fact that the millions of men and women around me are preoccupied with matters of another order invites me to remind them that they and their activities shall shortly or at length vanish from this globe, but that there is a way open for them leading to the eternal life which is enduring treasure.

Some will label me as of that dwindling crowd of dreamers who think to find a starry height in man. They will not be wrong, but I would beg them to realize that they can make my dream their own reality. The way I have followed may be aside from the common one, but it is not so far off that more cannot tread it also. If a foolish age calls us a band of mere dreamers, we at least have the consolation of knowing that we dream while they sleep in dire spiritual unconsciousness.

Others will ask: "Can this Light be followed in the midst of present-day sorrows and sufferings?" To them I would say: "This is precisely the time when its divine worth can best be proved."

There are certain essential truths about life, certain fundamental and unalterable principles which govern living, which have been known to the wise of all ages from the farthest antiquity till the present day. Healing can be found for *all*. No man is so broken, so oppressed by burdens of ill-health, poverty and unhappiness, but there is some way out of or around his problem, or in the last resort some way to bear it. This is so, this must be so, because all men exist *within* the Universal Mind which has brought this world into being—a Mind which is perennially benevolent, unfathomably wise and eternally peaceful. There are ugly things in the social life around us which may appear to contradict the latter statement, but the man who is willing to make the effort and unfold his spiritual insight, will discover that the statement is a true one, all appearances to the contrary. The least result of continued effort along the lines laid down in this book will be that the practitioner will become established in an inner peace which must mark him out from his fellows as a man of envied poise. And after he has found this peace other people will come to him, both young and old, and question him for the secret which seems to have eluded them. And then he in his turn will show them the Way. . . .

## CHAPTER II

### MAN—SCIENCE'S GREATEST RIDDLE!

"Know then thyself, presume not God to scan,
The proper study of mankind is man.
Plac'd on this isthmus of a middle state,
A being darkly wise, and rudely great:
With too much knowledge for the Sceptic side,
With too much weakness for the Stoic's pride,
He hangs between; in doubt to act, or rest;
In doubt to deem himself a god, or beast;
In doubt his mind or body to prefer;
Born but to die, and reasoning but to err;

                .          .          .

Sole judge of truth, in endless error hurl'd,
The glory, jest and riddle of the world!"
                                POPE's *Essay on Man.*

THE philosopher sits in the gallery of the Theatre of Life, looking down upon the play being enacted on the distant stage. It may be this exteriorized position which enables him to pass adequate judgments upon it all. Those who sit in the stalls at the Passing Show of This World have a nearer view than those who sit in the gallery, but they do not necessarily take a truer view of the play.

The mysterious meaning of life means nothing to us! We do not permit such a problem to take entry into our consciousness. We like to relegate such an inquiry to philosophical old fogeys or credulous old clergymen. The search for truth has become a bore. That which should provide us with a happy purpose, is an unspeakable occupation and an unpardonable subject in polite society.

God writes His message on the face of this round planet. Man, being self-blinded, is unable to read it. A few, having sight, interpret it to the others. But the human mass sneers at them for their pains, only the intuitive few among the cultured and intelligent and the child-like simple ones among the peasants and workers, receive the message and return love to the messengers. Therefore it is that the story of man's later history is red with tears and tragedy. But the complete story of humanity is neither a tragedy nor a comedy; no curtain falls nor is there an end.

Yes, mankind seems stricken with spiritual blindness and deafness. Unable to read the mystic writing on the wall of this world, unwilling to listen to the few seers who can do this, we pass through our days stumbling and groping. Uttered warnings or wise counsel—we dismiss such as the fervid vapourings of cranks, just as the Jews dismissed Christ's pointed truths. In the result men wander helplessly amid the bewildering chaos of to-day. We rise from the cradle of birth and grasp at life with passionate hands, but soon sink back into the passionless grave.

Our little selves are all-absorbed with the importance of our struggles and aspirations, our triumphs and defeats. Our luring possessions hold us captive, and we fret or fever ourselves on their account. We cannot help that, for we are human. But the Sphinx, rising out of Egyptian sands and surveying the mortal race of men, smiles . . . and smiles . . . and smiles!

Yet man is a rational being and instinctively craves for a rational explanation of things. He lives in a predominantly scientific and intellectual age. All his experience is interpreted by the light of a purely materialistic reason. But life appears to draw a hard line upon the map of his own nature, leaving a vast unknown land where Reason seems unable to penetrate. Reading in one of Bertrand Russell's old essays his fine but pessimistic confession of faith, I take it as typical of the sterile attitude forced upon those scientists who refuse all hope of ever exploring the unknown land. He wrote: "That man is the product of causes which had no prevision of the end they were achieving; that his origin, his growth, his hopes and fears, his loves and beliefs are but the outcome of accidental collocations of atoms; that no fire, no heroism, no intensity of thought and feeling can preserve an individual life beyond the grave; that all the labours of the ages, all the devotion, all the inspiration, all the noonday brightness of human genius, are destined to extinction in the vast depth of the solar system—all these things, if not quite beyond dispute, are yet so nearly certain that no philosophy which rejects them can hope to stand."

Such are the pessimistic thoughts which find tongue to-day among the intellectuals of our race. We can see the achievements of the scientists all around us in the world to-day; we must always admire their developed intellectuality; but yet they can only teach us the A B C of life: they do not know the X Y Z of it. Most of them are now frank enough to admit this, to confess their ignorance of the primal causes.

Those who would have us fall back on common sense in these matters wish us to fall back on a pitiful reed. They forget that common sense, in so far as it is merely the general uninstructed opinion, is sometimes synonymous with common ignorance.

Where then can we go to learn the first letters of Life's alphabet? We must go where humanity has always gone, where alone it can go. We must go to the Seers and Sages. Whilst the scientists have been searching the material universe for fresh facts, the Seers have been searching their own selves and exploring their own minds for old truths; for they have come to realize that they can but recover the ancient wisdom of man. What the first Seer found and recorded thousands of years ago, the last Seer finds and agrees with to-day. But what the first scientist of the nineteenth century found and recorded, the last scientist of to-day laughs at and flings aside. The latest results of science have already laid the frigid speculations of mid-Victorian scientists in a deep tomb. Yet the scientist is so sainted by the race to-day that unless and until he nods approval to each separate revelation of the Seer—a process which has been going on under our very eyes this last half-century—the pearl is thrown to the dust as false. Living scientists who can hardly be called dreamers now lend their names to the ideas of the Seers.

Bishop Berkeley's major doctrine was a similar view to that of the Indian Absolutists. He asserted that all we know of the world is our reaction to it, our impressions of it. He made mind the measuring-rod of the reality of our universe and hence placed mind as the first and fundamental reality. Sir James Jeans, by some brilliant efforts, has shown how physical science, working from the idea that the material world is the basic reality, has nevertheless been forced to consider favourably this hypothesis of Berkeley's. The conclusions of Einstein and Whitehead have similarly helped to confirm the Bishop's assertion.

Jeans writes in *The Mysterious Universe;* "All those bodies which compose the mighty frame of the world have not any substance without the mind." This Berkeleian conclusion is again reinforced by Sir Arthur Eddington, the eminent physicist, who likewise pictures the universe as an idea in the mind of—God! He even denies "actuality" apart from consciousness. Sir Oliver Lodge's work in physics, as well as his investigation into spiritualism, also points to man's mind as the reality in a world of vanishing matter. Our disdainful materialists dismiss this idea with a snap of their fingers. Those scientists who do accept it, become, in colloquial language, "cranks." It is noteworthy, however, that the latter are in the foremost ranks of their profession, and have been led to acceptance only after prolonged and profound research. One may make a little prophecy and declare that the whole army of scientists is unconsciously treading in this direction.

But we must free ourselves from the self-deception that the personality possesses a true standard of consciousness. We must first create within ourselves a true humility before we can know the liberating TRUTH. We must enter with Descartes, the clever Frenchman, into that frame of mind wherein he began one of his works: "I have held much to be true, which I now discover to be false; I have no reason to suppose anything to be more certain. Possibly everything that I conceive and believe is false. What then is true; what is certain?"

Thus the old mechanistic conception of life which was established by the founders of modern science from the seventeenth century onwards has begun to die out in the laboratory and lecture-room. The physicists themselves— once the proponents of the gospel of matter—have now become uncomfortably uncertain of physical phenomena. Their extended researches have shown them that what they once called inanimate matter can display certain properties which the text-books lay down as hitherto considered peculiar to the organic alone. This is the tragedy of time—it tests all things and ideas and proves again and again the falsity of the current conceptions of the moment.

§

When the craft of science took the winds of the seventeenth century with Bacon's carefully prepared compass, its crew would have been astounded had they been told in what strange waters it would be sailing in the nineteen-thirties. For the ship is bearing down on the harbour of those early philosophers who declared that time hardly has a separate existence, apart from the human brain; and that matter is the holding together of myriads of infinitesimal particles in an all-pervading ether.

Nineteenth-century science pedestalled the theory that life is a product of matter. Twentieth-century science is rapidly effecting a *volte-face* and is watching matter dissolve into electrons, into a mere collection of electrified particles, which elude sight and sense! The step from this stage into the matterless world beyond is not such a far one—intellectually.

Philosophy, once a sneered-at Cinderella, is now beginning to come into her own. Brilliant scientists like Jeans and Eddington have shown the inability of physical science to arrive at the nature of things without her help.

If we survey the course of scientific and philosophic thought since the year 1859 when Darwin published his epochal *Origin of Species,* we may trace its descent deep into materialism during the last century, and its ascent towards a more spiritual interpretation of the universe during this century.

The materialists who talk a mid-Victorian language in

Darwinian accents are becoming unintelligible to the brighter generation of to-day, who have followed science into the strange findings of Jeans and Einstein and Lodge.

When Einstein showed what a weird twist the sun's rays undergo before reaching our globe, the scientific lights which were guiding us dimmed a little and men grew wary of jumping to conclude the obvious. So, too, the psychology of fifty years ago looks a little woeful at the present time. The studies in abnormal psychology alone have played havoc with the seemingly sound explanations of that time.

The new order of scientific inquirers who now concern themselves with problems of time and causality, especially the mathematical physicists, have opened up entirely new vistas.

Einstein has also taught us to look upon time as another dimension, though we have hardly grasped the full import of this revolutionary idea. And if his later work is leading him anywhere, it is leading him to regard mind as the ultimate reality.

We live in an age of applied science: knowledge comes first; belief is but secondary. We probe every fact or event in this world with a searching "Why?" There is a cause for every visible effect. The old times when a baffling event was explained by a reference to the Will of God, or to the fiat of an angel, are gone, and gone for good. Spiritual truth must henceforth stand upon a scientific foundation; it must never be afraid of any question, and it must not dismiss the honest investigator as irreligious because he wants proof before he will believe.

During the closing decades of the eighteenth century, and the opening decades of the nineteenth, a constellation of literary and scientific luminaries appeared in the European sky which indicated and inaugurated the Age of Reason. God was dethroned and Reason became the throned sovereign of philosophy. Now science receives our highest worship. The scientist is the pope of to-day and sits in the Vatican of world authority. We receive his learned revelations in a spirit of religious awe. We trust his pontifical pronouncements as once nearly all Europe trusted the creeds and dogmas of the Church.

It is not the purpose of these thoughts to decry science, to cast contempt upon that vast structure of patiently acquired facts. I possess a profound respect for the intellectual abilities and patient character of the scientist. I believe his work has its right and useful place in life. But I do not believe that that place is the highest.

The practical utility of the scientific method is not to be deprecated. Only the fool will scorn the wonders which science has given man, though we would do well to pause and remember Disraeli's perceptive remark that: "The European talks of progress because by the aid of a few scientific discoveries he has established a society which has mistaken comfort for civilization." The fact that the scientist has confined his attentions to the objective world does not reduce the value of his discoveries. He has but to turn his attention inwards, to use the same methods of experiment and deduction upon the subjective world, to turn his searchlight of investigation towards the centre of his own mind, and he will penetrate the sphere of the spiritual.

Science has made the strides of a giant, but all her steps are in one direction—outwards, ever outwards. This is as it should be. Now the time has come to put an inside to her discoveries, to ensoul the forms she has created.

Is the soul a mere academic concept, an intellectual plaything for the professors to accept or deny? Is it only something upon which theologians may victoriously sustain their theses, and at which rationalists may fire their verbal shrapnel? At present the scientist can find no chemical trace of the soul; he cannot make it register on any of his instruments as he can make a gas register. But if chemical and mechanical reactions cannot be obtained, he need not therefore give up the quest baffled. Another way lies open. It may not be a conventional way, but it leads to the same objective—the discovery of the soul. If he loves truth better than convention, if he values the understanding of human life more than he values the understanding of a bit of rock, he will investigate that way. The method I propose to give is an extremely ancient one and goes so far back in man's history that its origin is lost in the dim mists of antiquity. Yet let not this fact be a charge against it. For the ancients were giants in the understanding of spiritual mysteries, but infants in the study of physical science: the moderns are masters in the development of physical science, but novices in the understanding of spiritual mysteries.

§

The great German philospher Kant said that there were two outstanding wonders of God's creation. He said these were the starry heavens above and the mind of man within. Great as are the exploits of science in the external world, greater discoveries yet await it this century in the domain of psychology. Man will draw back startled, when he understands the mysterious processes which occur within those inverted bowls of bone we call skulls!

Psychology, the science of mind and the study of consciousness, offers the most valuable rewards to true scientific research. No other subject is understood so little yet means so much, for it holds the key to man's deeper happiness.

Time will necessarily lift the idea of the soul out of the limbo of discarded theological notions into the grouping of scientifically tested propositions. But the science of that day will perhaps be as ready to utilize the mind as an experimenting instrument as to-day it uses the microscope. What are now regarded as the foolish illusions of mystics will then be the verified truths of the science of parapsychology, to be publicly proclaimed without reserve.

That the twentieth century will unveil somewhat of this mystery who that has followed the gropings of science can doubt. During its very first decade, the penetrating brain of the French thinker, Bergson, flashed the following prophetic message to his pen: "To explore the most sacred depths of the unconscious, to labour in the subsoil of consciousness: that will be the principal task of psychology in the century which is opening. I do not doubt that wonderful discoveries await it there."

A leading scientist like Eddington tells us that the physical universe is an abstraction if it is not linked with consciousness. Mind is no longer to be regarded as a mere by-product evolved by matter. The next and obvious step is to investigate the phenomena of consciousness, an investigation which was ridiculed a half-century ago by Huxley, because he regarded such phenomena as mere shadows attached to the real phenomena.

This internal exploration is well worth while. For there is something within the mind of man and beast, something that is neither intellect nor feeling, but deeper than both, to which the name of intuition may fitly be given. When science can truly explain why a horse will take its drunken rider or driver for miles through the dark and find its own way home; why field-mice seal up their holes before the cold weather comes; why sheep move away to the lee side of a mountain before severe storms; when it can tell us what warns the tortoise to retire to rest and refuge before every shower of rain; and when it can really explain who guides a vulture many miles distant to the dead body of an animal, we may then learn that intuition is sometimes a better guide than intellect. Science has wrested from the clasp of Nature some astonishing secrets, but thus far it has not discovered the source of intuition.

Intellect, which is able to propound a multitude of enigmas concerning man, destiny and death, is unable to solve them. When science shall have conquered the world, and the last glimmer of the last mystery shall have died out, it will still be faced with the greatest of all problems: "Man, dost thou understand thyself?"

I would like to have lived in Athens at the time when one could wander into the market-place and hear a certain snub-nosed, pugnacious man, one Socrates, cross-question the public men of the city, and repeatedly pose them this favourite question of his. A man like Socrates does not die and his sublime character outlives the grave.

When all the latest literatures have been examined and all the earliest papyrii have been exhumed, we shall find no wiser precept than the Delphic Oracle's injunction, "Know thyself!" and the Indian Rishees' counsel to "Inquire into the Self." These words, though older than the mummies in the British Museum, might have come from the typewriter of a modern thinker. The ages cannot kill a truth, and the first man who phrased it will find his echo right down through the centuries.

§

We live on a whirling ball in space, positioned somewhere in the great sky between the star of Venus and the star of Mars. There is something in this for man to think about and something at which to laugh. He has measured with undeniable accuracy the mileage between his own planet and the two stars, although the distances are so tremendous as to beggar imagination, yet he is unable to measure the extent of his own mind! He is a mystery to himself, a mystery which remains unsolved even when death's bitter waters come lapping to his feet.

Is it not ironical that the soul of man should seem less open to investigation than the earth on which he abides? Is it not passing strange that he should have been too busy with the world without to have troubled his mind about the world within until lately?

Why should he worry how the universe works? He does not have to run it, anyhow. But he does have to run himself.

> "The solar system turns without thine aid,
>   Live, die! The universe is not afraid,"

wrote that clever thinker, Zangwill.

Man, however, hardly appreciates this pointed truth.

He knows more about the workings of an automobile than he knows about the workings of his inner self. Yet the ancients taught—and a few of us have confirmed their teaching—that there is a stratum of his consciousness which bears the richest vein of all—pure gold. Should he not make this his chief concern?

Compared with its other results, modern science has discovered very little about the nature of man, even though it has discovered how to harden metals, how to drive a half-ton shell into the next city, and a hundred lesser things. During the last three centuries man's knowledge of the physical world has grown with amazing acceleration, but his knowledge of himself lingers far behind.

We can build giant bridges to span rivers of monstrous width, but we are unable to span the simple problem of "Who am I?" Our railway engines will traverse a whole continent with ease, but our minds cannot traverse the mystery of self. The astronomer brings the farthest star to the sight of his observatory, but he himself will bow his head in shame if you ask him whether he has brought his passions under complete control. We are full of curiosity concerning our planet, but we walk indifferently by at the mention of self.

We have gathered highly detailed information about

almost everything under the sun; we know the work, qualities and properties of almost all the objects and phenomena of this earth.

But we do not know our selves.

The very persons who have been studying all the sciences have yet to study the science of self; the very men who have discovered the why and wherefore of the lives of tiny insects do not know the why and wherefore of their own lives. We know the value of everything, but we do not know our own wonderful value.

We have packed the encyclopædias with thousands of pages concerning thousands of things, but who can write an encyclopædia about the mystery of his own self?

Why is it that the thing which interests every man most is—himself?

Because self is the only reality of which we are certain. All facts of the world around us and all thoughts in the world within us exist for us only when our own self becomes aware of them. Self sees the earth and earth exists. Self is conscious of an idea and the idea exists. Berkeley, by the process of acute thinking, arrived at the same position. He showed that the material world would be non-existent apart from some mind to perceive it.

What, then, is self?

There is no secret in the mysterious book of Nature which, with time and patience, cannot be read. No lock has been made but has its fitting key, and we may oft judge the handicraft of Nature by the handicraft of man.

The study of the self will one day prove the master-key to open all philosophical doors, all scientific conundrums, all life's locked problems. Self is the ultimate—it is the first thing we know as babes; it will be the last thing we shall know as sages.

The greatest certainty in knowledge comes only in the sphere of self. We can know the world and its objects only through instruments and our senses; but that which reads those instruments and uses those senses is the self. Therefore we are beaten back to this position in the end, that the study of self is the most important study to which any thinker can give his mind.

A Sophist approached one of the Wise Men of ancient Greece, and thought to puzzle him with the most perplexing questions. But the Sage of Miletus was equal to the test for he replied to them all, without the least hesitation yet with the utmost exactitude.

1. What is the oldest of all things?
*"God,* because He has always existed."

2. What is the most beautiful of all things?
*"The Universe,* because it is the work of God."

3. What is the greatest of all things?
*"Space,* because it contains all that has been created."

4. What is the most constant of all things?
*"Hope,* because it still remains with man, after he has lost everything else."

5. What is the best of all things?
*"Virtue,* because without it there is nothing good."

6. What is the quickest of all things?
*"Thought,* because in less than a minute it can fly to the end of the universe."

7. What is the strongest of all things?
*"Necessity,* which makes man face all the dangers of life."

8. What is the easiest of all things?
*"To give Advice."*

But when it came to the ninth question our sage pronounced a paradox. He gave an answer which I am certain his worldly wise querent never understood, and which to most people will give only the most superficial meaning.

The question was:

What is the most difficult of all things?

And the Miletian sage replied:

*"To know Thyself!"*

This was the bidding to ignorant man from the ancient sages; this shall be the bidding yet.

## CHAPTER III

"Remote, yet near, unutterably aged, lone,
    He sits within the temple's inner shrine,
    With folded hands and countenance divine,
Omniscient, inscrutable, unknown."

                                        G. P. WILLIAMSON.

SAINTS and sages, thinkers and philosophers, priests and scientific inquirers have tried for centuries to understand the enigmatic nature of the human soul. They find man a paradoxical being; one capable of descent into the darkest abysses of evil, and yet equally capable of ascent to the sublimest heights of nobility. They discover two creatures within his breast—one related to the demons and the other related to the angels. So wonderfully constituted is man that he can develop out of his own nature all that is most admirable equally with all that is most reprehensible in life.

Are we mere lumps of animated matter? Has man no higher birth than the flesh?

Or are we spirit-entities, bright and radiant from God, but temporarily housed and limited in our bodies?

Are we, as many think, nothing more than improved monkeys, ex-apes with ugly traits that betray our lineage, or are we, as a few believe, nothing less than degenerate angels?

Are we to be the hapless prey of Time? Is each of us to fill his obscure corner of this earth for a brief while and then disappear?

"When I look abroad, on every side I see dispute, contradiction, distraction. When I turn my eye inwards, I find nothing but doubt and ignorance. What am I? From what cause do I derive my existence? To what condition shall I return? I am confounded with these questions. I begin to fancy myself environed with the deepest darkness on every side," wrote the Scotch sceptical thinker, David Hume.

Is it possible for us to find the true answers to these perplexing questions? Man flings these questions at the face of life, and waits . . . and waits . . . but finds no answer till he totters into the grave. Yet the gods have invested man with intelligence, a faculty which is fully equal to discovering the truth about his own self, though it may fail when confronted by the deeper riddle of the universe.

These are the riddles of life which have puzzled the sages of sixty generations, and will puzzle many more. The cleverest minds, the ablest pens and the most eloquent lips have busied themselves with these dark enigmas, but still mankind gropes for the answers.

Man—a doubting and despairing figure—stalks across the cold wastes of this world and laughs cynically at the name of God. But despair is the stricken child of ignorance.

God has sent a true light into the heart of every child that is born, but it must be unveiled. We have wrapped around it the dark shrouds that blind us, and we ourselves must unwrap them. No cry that goes up from the depths of a sincere heart goes up in vain, and if your prayer is fashioned aright, it will be answered by the god in your own heart.

The average man sends out his tentacles towards Life, feeling his way towards something he does not quite comprehend. He has hardly perceived that when he begins to apply his intelligence to the solution of his own problem— himself—he will automatically solve the parallel problems of God, Life, the Soul, Happiness, and so on.

The white race has wandered all over the surface of this earth in search of new Americas till there is hardly a rod of land upon which it has not set foot. Yet I purpose to indicate here another world, which has indeed been explored by a few, but ignored by many. It is not so very long ago that our geographers denied the existence of a goodly part of this world that they inhabited; the spacious concept of America was once placed among the things at which to laugh loudly.

So, too, it has been the case with the common notion that what we can at present see of man—his fleshly form— represents all that he is and all that we are ever likely to be. The worms will hold high revel over the sum total of ourselves, and not merely over our bodies. The notion is a nasty one, but many, if not most people, consider it a true one and regard the possibility of surviving death as something to be ridiculed. They shake their heads and profess that they cannot understand the mystery of spirit, but they will readily accept matter, whose ultimate nature is hardly less mysterious. It is part of my purpose to show that such persons go wrong when they make the mistake of accepting the common condition of human mentality as representing its ultimate. It is true that there are slimy trails in man dark with the creeping of strange and vile creatures. But then there are also radiant places where the soul swiftly takes wings. The psychoanalyst who looks only for the first —finds them!

§

Throughout the verbal traditions handed down by our earlier forefathers, and shining through the literature of the world, far back as the first rude manuscripts of Oriental peoples and up to the newest product of the printer's press of this year of grace, there has been a strange yet recurring allusion to another self within man. It does not matter what name was given to this mysterious self, whether it be called soul or breath, spirit or ghost. There is, indeed, no other doctrine in the world which possesses so far-flung an intellectual ancestry as this.

Everybody knows that there is a fixed limit to the range within which normal human consciousness can function. Everybody does not know that there have always been some intrepid humans who have played the King Canute to their own minds—bidding the turbulent waves of thought roll back until consciousness crossed the normal limit and found itself in the free worlds of the spirit.

These statements of experience made by spiritual Seers throughout the ages must be faced. They are either the babblings of irresponsible lunatics, or they are words of such importance as to upset the present materialistic basis of our life.

I do not know that it will avail us much trying to trace out the paternity of this doctrine, for truth may arise in a multitude of heads all over the globe and none be its primal father save the mysterious Source whence all thought takes its rise. We can sometimes learn truer lessons by studying Nature than by studying books. A man once sat and watched a worm bore a hole through a piece of wood. This simple observation taught him the principle of boring tunnels. To-day, because of this man's insight, trains run under wide rivers and through mountains of solid rock. . . . So the first Seers, watching the wanderings of thought within their own minds, discovered that there was something which came into action when thinking momentarily stopped. That Something was the first faint intimation of the soul. Thus the science of soul-discovery was born and the ancients began to teach men how to know the truth about themselves.

In almost every pre-Christian civilization this knowledge was communicated in various ways, in Sumeria, Babylon, Chaldea, China, Persia, India, Mexico, among the North American Indians, the Central American Mayas and the ill-fated Aztecs; by the Essenic fraternity among the Jews and by the Gnostics of East Mediterranean cities.

Amid the majestic ruins which strew the face of present-day Greece there stands a vast roofless structure of tumbling walls and broken columns. They are all that is left of the site where once the festivals of the Eleusinian Mysteries were celebrated in pomp and reverence under the ægis of Athens. There are few to-day who understand what went on behind the walls of this sanctuary. Initiation into these Mysteries was esteemed a subject of high importance among the ancients, though we moderns hardly know what it means. Men like Macedonian Alexander and Roman Julius Cæsar did not hesitate to avail themselves of this sublime and unforgettable experience, and emerged to fulfil more consciously the great parts which destiny had allotted them, such was the grandeur of the knowledge which came to them behind closed and guarded doors.

When the epiphanies of the Greek Mysteries were concluded, the last words heard by the initiate were: *"Go in peace!"* And it is written by those who were themselves initiated that ever after he went his way through life with a soul at rest and mind serene. Initiation was really nothing more than to enter into an awareness of what the candidate really was. It completed the make-up of man and anyone who had not experienced it was really but a half-man. Something, some broken fragments of what he learnt in those old temples I have put into this book, but I have attempted to formulate these hoary old truths in language which will appeal to modern people, and to apply them to practical life. The key to the whole problem of this ancient Mystery-Institution was given by Plutarch when he wrote: "At the moment of death the soul experiences the same impressions as those who are initiated into the great Mysteries."

Scholars are likewise uncertain as to the real purport of the Great Pyramid, that vast building whose interior mirrors the eternal quiet of the yellow deserts of Egypt. Because in its later days the funerary rites of the Pharaohs were celebrated there, they arrive at the mistaken but natural conclusion that this marvellous structure was planned by its builders as a gigantic tomb. Its true purpose was infinitely higher than that. Here were brought candidates for the mystic experience called initiation, an experience wherein they were enabled to obtain temporary release from the limitations of the body and to contact this other self within man, among other things. This experience was brought about by external agency, by means of the powerful help of the high priests of that time.

Go to the British Museum and you will see a gigantic stone figure, brought there many years ago by a sailing ship from Easter Island, off the coast of South America. Examine the reverse side of this statue and you will see the clearly cut figure of *a handled cross*. It is identical with the Cross of Life, or Crux Ansata, so often shown in ancient Egyptian representations as being carried by their deities in their hands, and so often referred to as *the key to the Mysteries*. This is not merely a coincidence, but a significant pointer to the fact that the Mystery initiations were not unknown across the Atlantic.

There exists in Central America an almost exactly similar structure to the Egyptian Pyramid, and one which was used by the ancients for exactly similar purposes. The mysterious events which took place in the one were duplicated in the other, and what occurred in the Greek Eleusinian Temple was not dissimilar in its results to the results of both. There were several grades of initiation, naturally, but the candidates who succeeded in passing even the first had a new world of being temporarily opened to them and went back to the world as changed men and women, for they had temporarily touched their hidden selves.

If this interior experience was possible in the twentieth

century B.C. it is also possible in the twentieth century A.D. The *fundamental* nature of man has not changed during the interval. It is true, however, that the experience was easier found and more often attained in the earlier days because then life was more leisurely and less complicated.

Is this secret self nothing more than the wild fancy or vague chimera of a few but famous men about whom time and history tell us? Has this long chain of spiritual tradition no links that are made of stronger substance than superstition? Yet these riddles which baffle us must have baffled Babylon—to take a single example of an early civilization—too. If there were thinking men of that epoch who arrived at some kind of a solution which agrees in essence with that which was arrived at by thinking men of India, China, Egypt, Greece and Rome, it might be worth our while to investigate that solution. The result of such an investigation will be either to strengthen our present position and to weaken theirs, or to weaken our own dearly cherished beliefs and to confirm the doctrines of the ancients. And the only sort of investigation which is of any use to this inquiry is a practical one.

I have taken the trouble to carry out such a research, though not without some difficulty, and in the sequence have been compelled to testify that the wisdom of the ancients is not altogether a fanciful thing. Indeed, I have discovered that their doctrines, instead of being the unreal coinage of dreamers' heads, contain much in which we who live and work in the bustling world may place credence.

The modern mind does not care to resort to the famous thinkers of antiquity to have its problems solved. Thereby it misses much. It may be that the meditations of these sages of antiquity can yield not a little fruit for the students of modernity. We may attempt to cut ourselves adrift from the great philosophies of the past, but, since they were based on the eternal principles upon which all true thinking must be based, we shall be forced to return. Philosophy fell from power when the over-intellectual reduced it to mere disputation; it will be restored to its rightful place when the over-sophisticated souls of to-day awake to the need of a more enlightened outlook than the present confused teaching can afford.

There is something more in man than is apparent from ordinary impressions. The discoveries of abnormal psychology throw out strange hints about this, and the never-ending accounts of mystical experience confirm it. What is this "moreness" in man which causes him to hold fine ideals and to foster great thoughts? What is this finer spiritual presence in his heart which fitfully pulls him away from a merely earthly existence, thus setting up constant strife between the angel and the beast which tenant our body?

When we moderns are told that God is not a mere word to be argued and debated about but a state of consciousness we can realize here and now in the flesh, we raise our eyebrows; when some spiritual Seer quietly tells us that there are God-knowing men living among us now, we significantly tap our foreheads. When, further, we are assured that we bear the divine within our breasts and that divinity constitutes our true selfhood, we smile in a superior way.

Yet this is not theory nor is it sentiment; it is an open and patent fact to people who have gone some way in spiritual percipiency.

Before the calm Sphinx of a truly spiritual teaching, the West stares blankly. It can make the most amazing machines; it can build ships of stupendous size; it can transform our homes with the wonders of wireless and applied electricity; yet it cannot do this simple thing—it cannot receive and understand the meaning of life. The plain fact is that calamity has fallen upon us and we have forgotten who we are. We can trace our kin to the ape, with a wealth of detail and proof for this miserable pedigree, but we cannot remember our kindred with the angel.

We have been too content with allocating the high places of spirituality to the few names of a far-off past, and with assigning the muddy depths to humanity in general. We forget our own divine nature. For we too can approach Jesus, become Buddha-like or win the wisdom of a Plato. Yet unless we believe this passionately, we shall remain sunk to a status near the animals,

> "But what thing dost thou now,
>     Looking Godward, to cry,
>  'I am I, thou art thou,
>     I am low, thou art high?'
> I am thou, whom thou seekest to find him.
>     Find thou but thyself, thou art I.

.        .        .

O my sons, O too dutiful
Towards Gods not of me,
Was not I enough beautiful?
Was it hard to be free?
For behold, I am with you and in you and
of you; look forth now, and see."

*Hertha*, by ALGERNON C. SWINBURNE.

§

There are those who will express disdain at this ego-centric philosophy. Them I shall answer, not with my own words, but with inspired announcement of the German seer, Eckhardt, "*God is at the centre of man.*"

Does one blaspheme against God in thus deifying the self? Only the superficial can make this accusation. For the true soul of man is Divinity; there can be no blasphemy in such an attitude.

We have nearly forgotten the existence of the spiritual self, though the self, in its long-waiting vigil, will never forget us.

Why has man possessed the religious yearning? Because we love ourselves, because we unconsciously yearn for union with our true selves.

The human race possesses an age which defies imagination. Countless figures of men, women and children have appeared upon this turning planet through æons of time, and having played their parts seem to have sunk down to eternal sleep. The keenest intellects of our time are busy gathering the materials left by the races of yesterday, the upheaval vestiges of ancient civilizations and the secrets of a cataclysmic past, yet the Seer must smile at their admirable but pathetic efforts to take intellectual toll of an ancestry which is infinitely outstretched. In the picturesque words of Sulpicius to Cicero: "All things are being precipitated by the relentless decree of an immutable Fate down the yawning throat of everlasting oblivion."

If we follow the seers and fling the æons aside, peering into the dimmest regions of prehistoric antiquity, we reach a period when man entirely dropped his body of flesh and inhabited an electromagnetic form, a radiant body of ether. Farther back there was a change in his inner nature, and he dropped off all passions and personal emotions entirely, all feelings or desires like fear, anger, hatred, lust and the like. But thoughts still played in his consciousness, still arose like waves upon the surface of his mind and still connected themselves with his *personal* life. And so we trace him back to a time when even thoughts took their exit and when the necessity of thinking in a sequential logical manner in order to obtain understanding, disappeared. Not only did he no longer need the reasoning faculty, but it even became a hindrance to him. For man had now reached the naked condition of pure Selfhood.

The whole matter might perhaps be put more plainly by saying that the human race, in the course of its long history, has superimposed a second self upon the individual nature with which each man began. This second self is usually called the person and came into being through a union of spirit and matter, through a commingling of particles of consciousness drawn from the ever-conscious real self with particles of unconscious matter drawn from the body. This second and later self is the one we each of us know, the personal self, but the first and real self, which existed before thinking and desiring appeared within the being of man, is the one which few of us know, which is subtle and not so apparent because it makes us all partake of the nature of divinity. It lives always over our heads, an angelic thing of unimaginable grandeur and mysterious sublimity, and therefore I call it the *Overself.*

Back of the man we see lives another man whom we do not see. Back of this body of flesh is a starry and sublime consciousness.

This doctrine of the true self in man is expressed beautifully by one of India's ancient seers: "Unseen but seeing, unheard but hearing, unperceived but perceiving, unknown but knowing. . . . This is thy Self, the ruler within, the immortal."

The materialist never tires of telling us how foolish the pale visionary is for trying to catch clouds; and the Overself, sitting in the heart of the taunter, smiles tolerantly at all his logical twaddle.

We live our true lives in the depths of our hearts, not in the superficial mask of personality which we show the world. The living inhabitant is more important than the stone house.

Walt Whitman, that bluff and enthusiastic Yankee rhymeless poet, saw this truth in his half-confused manner, and expressed it thus in *Leaves of Grass:*

"I swear I begin to see the meaning of these things.
It is not the earth, it is not America, who is so great,
It is I who am great or to be great. . . .

Underneath all, individuals.
I swear nothing is good to me now that ignores individuals. . . .

The whole theory of the universe is directed unerringly to one single individual—namely to You."

And this from Whitman's poem *To You:*

"O I could sing such grandeurs and glories about you!
You have not known what you are, you have slumbered upon yourself all your life.
The mockeries are not you;
Underneath them and within them I see you lurk.
Whoever you are, claim your own."

There are memorable moments in our lives when we receive from the Overself hints of a higher existence possible to man. At such times our house of life is unshuttered and slender rays of dawn enter in. We know then that the soul's dreams can come true, that Love and Truth and Happiness are indeed our birthright, but, alas! the brief hour passes and with it our faith. Are they then to be of no worth to us, those shining lapses into a diviner existence? Let them stand as "pillars of cloud by day, pillars of fire by night," to guide us through the wilderness of modern times.

These faint and impalpable intuitions which come to a man in his sanest moments are half-heard whispers of this greater Self of his. The spiritual call is forever trying to voice itself in the heart of mankind, but we do not listen. The spiritual impulses which arise in the hearts of our best men, are themselves the best token of a higher possibility for the race.

Man, as he really is, and as he eternally has been and shall be, is a spiritual being. Life in the physical body does not detract from the truth of this statement. The material senses hold man under a hypnotic glamour and, real enough in their own way, cause him to confound his true self with them. Heaven lies about us, not only during the innocent days of infancy, but every moment of existence, yet we know it not. A few are so close to this truth that they are unconsciously waiting for the miraculous moment of recognition. They have but to be told of it in the right way and hope will flash up in their souls. That hope is the silent voice of the Overself.

It is somewhat ironical that man's very self—his true nature—has become a secret in these days.

Man walks along the dusty roads of life like that seeker of old time who spent the years wandering through foreign lands in quest of a rare treasure of which he had heard, whilst all the time he himself was being sought for as the heir to a great fortune. Wrapped in the folds of our own nature hides a rare jewel, though we know it not. None has yet dared to set a price upon it, nor will any ever dare to do so, for its value is beyond all things of known worth.

We must try, then, to trace out the Overself, to run down the gamut of our inner workings till we can get no farther. Then we shall realize that body and intellect are not our be-all, but that the Overself is the witness of both, the source of complete peace, perfect intelligence and absolute immortality.

We of this practical century have little confidence in abstract propositions. We are always dubious about thoughts which carry us away from the concrete world. We distrust and deprecate theoretical systems which take their start out of the air.

The question will be asked: "Do you possess any practical method whereby we may attain this self-knowledge which you praise so much? Or is yours but a speculative doctrine which may make a nice adornment to the facade of metaphysics but is without utility to men who work, live, love and suffer? Is it but a dreamy fancy which cannot hold out against the grim actualities of modern city life?"

And so, without any more ado, I shall place before the reader a description of the way of investigation which he, too, may follow if he cares and which, carried to a successful issue, will answer convincingly the perplexing questions that troubled my head once and may now trouble his.

## CHAPTER IV

### THE PRACTICE OF MENTAL QUIET

THE sovereignty of nature has been allotted to the silent forces. The moon makes not the faintest echo of a noise, yet it draws millions of tons of tidal waters to and fro at its bidding. We do not hear the sun rise nor the planets set. So, too, the dawning of the greatest moment in a man's life comes quietly, with none to herald it to the world. In that stillness alone is born the knowledge of the Overself. The gliding of the mind's boat into the lagoon of the spirit is the gentlest thing I know; it is more hushed than the fall of eventide.

Only in deep silence may we hear the voice of the soul; argument but beclouds it and too much speech stops its appearance. When you have caught your fish you may share it, but while you are angling for it, talk breaks the spell and frightens the fish away. If we could occupy ourselves less with the activities of the larynx and more with the activities of the deeper mind, we might arrive at something worth saying. Speech is an adjunct, not an obligation. *To be* is the prime duty of man.

Life teaches us silently while men utter their instruction in loud voices.

The treasure-trove of the real self is within us, but it can be lifted only when the mind is still

Words hint at this Reality, but they do not, cannot explain it. Truth is a state of being, not a set of words. The cleverest argument is no substitute for personal realization. We must experiment if we are to experience. The word "God" is meaningless to me unless I can contact the Absolute within myself; then only can I place it in my vocabulary.

A little practice goes a long way. A score of lectures will not make plain to the sceptical senses, a hundred books cannot reveal to the inner sight what is discovered by those who faithfully and resolutely attempt the method outlined in these pages.

The so-called scientific and philosophic proofs of the Spiritual Reality prove nothing at all. The German philosopher Kant showed long ago that the reason cannot grasp this Reality. Hence all our "proofs" are mere piling-up of words. It is equally as easy to disprove this Reality on the strength of another set of evidences, or by the force of an opposing group of arguments, as it is to "prove" it.

Something of a thrill passed through the learned world when Einstein announced his discovery of the curvature of a ray of light passing near the sun. This observation was to establish his theory of Relativity, but at the time we all thought it might lead to much more than that. We thought that with a little more research along the same lines, and a little more speculation about the results of that research, the existence of God might be brought within the range of scientific proof. Alas! that eager anticipation, which filled so many minds and touched so many pious hearts, has receded somewhat during the years. Science can still deliver no certain verdict on this question.

The greatest problems of individual existence, the supreme questions which haunt the life of every earnest man, cannot be solved within the few inches which confine the human brain. But satisfying answers for them are waiting for us in the limitless interior of our being, in the divine substance of our hidden nature. For the brain can answer only with barren words, whereas the spirit answers with the ravishing experience of internal illumination. Whoever will earnestly put into regular practice the mystical concentration explained in this book, will receive increasing confirmation of the truth of man's divinity by his own first-hand experience. Books and bibles will begin to lose their authority as he begins to find his own.

God is His own best interpreter. Find the god in your own heart and you will understand by direct intuition what all the great teachers, real mystics, true philosophers and inspired men have been trying to tell you by the tortuous method of using words.

You cannot show my intellect that God, the Absolute, the Spirit—call it as you please—exists; but you can show this to me by changing my consciousness until it can participate in the consciousness of the God within me.

There is one way only to effect this change and at the same time discover who we really are. That way is to pass from the outer to the inner, from being busy with a multitude of external activities to being busy with a single internal activity of the mind.

St. Augustine soliloquizes thus: "I, Lord, went wandering like a strayed sheep, seeking Thee with anxious reasoning without, whilst thou wast within me . . . I went round the streets and squares of the city of this world seeking thee; and I found thee not, because in vain I sought without for him, who was within my self."

We must throw the plummet of mind into the depths of self. The deeper it falls the richer will be the treasure we shall recover from that calm Saragossan sea. Consciousness must be pivoted at the inmost point of one's being. Each man has a private door opening onto the eternal brightness. If he will not press and push it open, his darkness is self-doomed.

If you want proof of your divinity listen in to your Overself, for that proof is within you. Take a little time out of your leisure to shut out the tumultuous distractions of the world and enter into a short seclusion; then listen with patience and attention to the reports of your own mind in the manner which I shall shortly explain. Repeat this practice every day, and one day that proof will suddenly visit your solitude. And with it will come a glorious freedom when the burdens of man-made theologies or man-made scepticisms will go out from you. Learn to touch your Overself —and you will never again be drawn into those futile circles where men raise the dust of theological argument or make the noise of intellectual debate. In this way you will finally settle the question for yourself, independently of what any book may say about it, no matter how sacred or secular it be.

Some people call this meditation and indeed the word is as good as any, except that I propose to describe a method of meditation which differs in its basic principle from most of the methods which have been reported to me, and which might be more appropriately called *mental quiet*.

The only way to understand the meaning of meditation

is to practise it. "Four thousand volumes of metaphysics will not teach us what the soul is," exclaimed Voltaire.

Like most things that are worth while, the results of meditation are not arrived at except with labour and difficulty, but to those who practise aright they shall surely be reached. We begin by fitful experiment, and we end by divine experience. We play with meditation and try to contemplate, but a dawn will one day arise when our minds shall steep themselves in the endless beatitude of the Overself.

Meditation is almost a lost art in the West. Few practise it and even among these fewer still understand what they are doing. The habit of setting aside a little time each day for daily meditation, for daily quietening of the mind, is to-day noticeably conspicuous by its absence from the life of Western peoples. The hypnotic power of external existence clings to our minds as a leech clings to human flesh. The unwilling conscious self will bring dozens of good excuses against starting this practice or against continuing it after it has been started. The personality finds it dull, empty or too much of a strain. The initial battle of overcoming the brain's unwillingness to come to rest is perhaps the hardest, but it must be fought. Yet it is a habit of vital importance whose benefit, when practised, cannot be too highly exaggerated; but whose neglect leads to worry and woe.

Beyond the commonplace trivialities of the daily round, there is a finer and fairer existence.

However much we may resist this diviner claim upon us during the day, we are unable to resist returning to the inner self during deep dreamless sleep. Then we are captured by the soul; then we enjoy rest in our own nature, albeit unconsciously. It is an arresting thought, this, and a hint of high philosophic truth.

But how can a people enslaved by the trials and tumults of material life become aware of this wonderful truth? Therefore it is that those who are wise take up the daily practice of calming the mind and withdrawing it into the deep abiding peace that lies hidden within us.

General Gordon regularly set one hour aside every morning for his spiritual devotions; how much inspiration for his soldierly activities, how much strength and courage did he not draw from this wise practice?

William T. Stead, famous newspaper editor and fighter for the outcast, once spent three months in prison because he dared to publish the truth. He declared in after years that these were the most profitable months of his life. "It was the first time in my life that I had had time to sit down and think, to sit down *and find myself*," he said afterwards.

Thomas A. Edison, whose name will always be starred on the world's list of great inventors, developed through repeated habit the ability to relax in the midst of his work and throw himself into a meditative condition which brought him the solution of many of his perplexing problems. He once said: "The hours which I have spent alone with Mr. Edison have brought me the real big returns of my life; to it I attribute all I have accomplished."

We give no thought to the inner life. We try to persuade ourselves that we have not a half-hour to spend sitting by the quiet well of Truth. A moment of mental quiet is looked upon as a moment wasted. Hence the masses are not wiser for their multitude of days.

The modern world believes it has no use for such a thing as meditation, which too often is condemned as a mere abstraction. And the modern world is not altogether wrong nor altogether right in its usual attitude. History shows how religion, to take one example, has produced a number of meditative visionaries who invited others to enter with them into the domain of sheer self-delusion, and to wander into the realm of puerile fancies. It is such misguided persons who have been responsible for the common notion that spiritual seers are men who stand gazing into the heavens, exploring with their mental eyes dim cloudlands of no interest and of no use to saner mortals. They are the sham mystics who live in fantastic worlds of their own: what they need is a hard bump against reality.

But history also tells us of a band of seers who take higher rank. They were men of spotless character and exceptional charity. Their common characteristic was that they had passed through an experience which lit up their minds with untellable illumination and which bestowed ecstatic happiness. These were the true mystics, if you like. Their statements, which were phrased in all humility, revealed that they had penetrated to the inmost regions of man's heart; they had gone into that deeper place where the soul abides; and they had discovered at last the diviner nature of man,

which remains untouched and unfallen though tenemented
in frail flesh. It is not my purpose to list their names, but
the books of Evelyn Underhill and Dean Inge give a good
idea of the most important ones within the Christian fold.

The world's mind is too apt to become hypnotized by its
material environment. For many persons, the spiritual life
has become a mere myth. It is a strange and sad thing that
while our leading scientists and finest intellects are returning towards a more spiritual interpretation of the universe
and of life, the masses have sunk deeper into the gross
materialism which the first fumbling researches of science
appeared to justify.

So we ought to be somewhat grateful to those seers who
ventured into untrodden fields to bring back report of the
diviner life which is possible to man. True vision is a tremendous experience, not a set of theories. No man who has
lived through even a temporary spiritual experience is ever
likely to forget it. His days will be haunted until he sets
out to seek ways and means of repeating it.

§

I have no complicated system to formulate in these pages.
I propose only to teach a simple technique for becoming
aware of the highest in ourselves. No method of meditation
can be easy in itself, because the practice connotes thought-
control, than which few things are harder in this world. Yet
a method of meditation can, however, be simple. It need
not be complicated by tortuous paraphernalia, nor tied up
with a mind-beclouding jargon.

Various systems of meditation had been taught, different
paths of Yoga have been chalked out in both ancient and
modern times. The technique for attaining self-knowledge
which is propounded here, however, cannot be brought
easily into any of these existing classifications. This Art of
Interrogative Self-Reflection stands alone in its simplicity,
uniqueness, originality and power, although it naturally has
several points of contact with the other systems. I do not
claim that it offers the best path, but I do claim that it
offers a quicker and safer means of attaining spiritual self-
knowledge than most of the paths I know. The various
branches of Yoga, that profound but complicated Indian

way, are excellent when considered in relation to the people and epoch to whom they were given, but when considered in relation to the Western races and modern needs, they obviously prove too impracticable except for a few.

This inquiry into the true self is the simplest system of meditation I know, and therefore the most suited to the busy man of the present age. It is quicker to grasp and simpler to practise than the complicated Yoga systems of the East. It may advantageously be practised by anyone who cares to ascertain the truth about his own nature.

When you have awakened in the morning and bathed, the first duty—and usually the most neglected one—confronting you is to "plug in" to your true self. Yet most people make it their first duty to think of their present troubles, the work in hand or the persons they are soon to meet. Their activities and their problems are first in their thoughts, instead of obtaining that wisdom which should inspire all their activities and solve all their problems. When Jesus said: "Seek ye first the kingdom of heaven, and all these things shall be added unto you," He gave us not only a general rule, but also a particular one.

His use of the words "this day" in the Lord's Prayer is a significant indication that He advised His followers to pray or meditate in the morning. There exist deep psychological reasons for this counsel. We can set the keynote of the entire day's activities by the attitude adopted during the first hour after waking from sleep. The activities and desires of the day have not then begun to disturb the mind.

If we seek the kingdom first thing every morning, and sacrifice a little time for its sake, our work will not suffer and our problems will not be neglected. But thereby we create a current of spiritual wisdom and strength which will flow beneath the whole of the day's activities and thoughts. Whatever we do will be done correctly, whatever decision we must reach will be the right one because it will be the fruit of calmer, deeper thought. Those who think it folly to attend to our spiritual attitude before we have attended to our worldly concerns put second things first and first things second. For them, as the Hindu scripture puts it: "There is peace neither in this world nor the next."

Whether we give five minutes or five hours to this practice of life-inspiring, it never fails to produce remarkable rewards in the long run. Is it not worth a quarter to half an hour a day to find mental poise and the consciousness of inner mastery?

This matter of practising meditation for ten minutes to half an hour once or twice a day is merely one of habit, since a person gradually becomes accustomed to it as a part of his normal life. The second fortnight will be slightly easier, the third easier still, until in time you master the art. Even the busy man of affairs can fit it into his programme so that it becomes as natural as having his meal. Create the habit, stick to it, and without doubt it will begin to make its value felt in conscious progress.

Spiritual unfoldment is not to be the haphazard thing it so often is among us, but a steady and serious effort. An ordered and regular daily practice in meditation will naturally lead to advancement in the art. In other words, as you continue the method less and less effort will be needed to produce the same result. Progress depends upon practice.

Meditation will produce most results by being regular every day, rather than in fits and starts, because it is something that gradually "soaks in" by repeated daily efforts.

The daily practice of mental quiet must be done as regularly as eating. Habit rules our lives. The man who has learnt the secret of creating habits is able to control that which controls life. And the best habit a man can make is that of meditation. I would not only emphasize but overemphasize the astonishing value and urgent necessity of this habit. You will find in time that the daily period of mental quiet will become a looked-for joy, instead of a disciplinary duty, as it might seem at first, and you will allow nothing to interfere with it.

§

The next point to observe is that certain physiological and psychological conditions are advisable if success is to be attained with less difficulty. An easy body-posture assists to put the mind at ease. A body in discomfort tends to make the mind uneasy.

Physical stillness is the first gateway to mental stillness. A comfortable and convenient posture of the body rests the mind and enables one to begin the task of withdrawing within oneself. Go to the same quiet spot or room every day, occupy the same chair or sit on the same bed each time. Sit upright and do not recline on your back. Thus the body learns to respond automatically until it becomes non-resistant to the invading influence of the Soul.

Meditation is easier to perform and will bear a better fruit when right conditions are conformed to. Choose a time when you will not be disturbed, when things around you are quiet, when the stomach and digestive organs are at rest, when the body feels comfortable, when the weather is not stormy. If it is also possible, fill your best room with flowers and incense. Put only ennobling and colourful pictures upon its walls. Let those four walls prove a holy of holies to help you dwell awhile with diviner things, and try to keep that room for your own personal use, so far as that can be done, a place wherein to meditate and pray and to study the things of the spirit. Before long it will begin to bear the invisible impress of the diviner life so that as soon as you step into it the cares and worries of worldly existence will fall from you. Anyhow, choose a place where you can remain in uninterrupted seclusion, where there is no noise, where animals and insects cannot irritate you and where you feel harmonious and at peace. If you cannot get all these conditions, then get as much of them as you can.

The first rule then is to mark off a small fixed fragment of your daily life, when you can devote yourself untroubled and undisturbed to the practice of the necessary exercises. You may begin with ten minutes, but you will try to extend the period to a half-hour as soon as you feel that it can be done without undue strain. Half an hour per day is a long time for the average Western man to spend in meditation, and it is not advisable to attempt a lengthier period except under the supervision of a competent teacher.

I have suggested that the morning be chosen, but it is quite possible that circumstances exist which debar this time. In that case, the next best time is sunset, for then the mind can return more quickly to its interior quiet than it is able to do during the activity of the daytime. There is a mysterious quality in twilight which links it with the great spiritual currents that Nature releases in regular rhythm.

If the early evening is out of the question, then an alternative time would be just before retiring to rest at night.

Failing these three times, you must then avail yourself of whatever half-hour you can steal from the daily schedule.

The fragment of time which you have marked off for this higher purpose is to be used in a manner which completely detaches it from the other activities of the day. Instead of busying yourself with something that draws and fastens your attention upon external matters, you will try to let go of such matters and of other persons, to put them aside for the time being as though they never even existed, and to rule your thoughts and feelings with the ideal of inner calm as your goal. Hitherto you may have given all your attention to the world without. The man who would understand himself must reverse this process and periodically divert that attention to explore the world within.

He who would attempt to know his Overself must learn to retire into his mind as a tortoise retires into its shell. The attention which has hitherto been dissipated on a succession of external objects must now be concentrated on a single internal focus.

The path of concentration is simple to describe, but difficult to practise. All you have to do is but to abstract your mind from all other thoughts save this one line of reflection which you set down as the subject of your concentration— but try it!

Thought control is hard to attain. Its difficulty will astonish you. The brain will rise in mutiny. Like the sea the human mind is ceaselessly active. But it *can* be done.

At the centre of our being dwells this wonderful Self, but to reach it we must cut a channel through all the thought-debris which rings it in and which forces us to pay unceasing attention to the material world as the only reality.

We like to turn inwards and let the mind rest in itself— not in the physical sense world—about as much as we like to hear the morning alarm clock.

We moderns have begun to bridle Nature, but we have not learnt yet how to bridle ourselves. Thoughts hunt and harry us in endless packs; they torment us out of sleep at night, and fasten freely upon us throughout the day. If we could but learn the secret of their control and suppression, we could then enter upon a marvellous repose, a peace similar to that which Paul described as passing understanding.

For the five senses cling to the material world like glue; they yearn for contacts with it in the forms of things, people, books, amusements, travel, and activities of every kind. You can only kill the enemy in the moments when the senses are silent. When you think of going into mental rest, the senses immediately begin to object; they cry out against it. They say to you: "We want to stay in our own physical world which we know; we are afraid of this inner spiritual world of mystery and meditation. It is natural for us to cling to the physical world." And so they try their utmost to keep you attached to the material sphere; and that is the true reason why you think you dislike meditation or at any rate shirk it, when the time for it comes. It is the senses that dislike it—not you; therefore, fight them and try to rule them. Mental effort comes first, then comes mental quiet.

The mastery of mind is the mastery of self. The soul that can conquer the ever-rising spray of thoughts can put on its captain's uniform and bid its whole nature stand to order. The power to hold on to a train of thought with great tenacity, to grasp it with scorpionic claws and not let go is the power to concentrate and makes MEN. The masters of thought are the true masters of men. Are you weak in concentration? Then by a little practice every day you can become stronger. He who tries every day to do so, albeit for only half an hour, shall master his wandering thoughts in time.

*A Warning: When moral weaknesses are conjoined with mystical practices, the result is not elevation of the mind into spirituality but degeneration of the mind into psychism. The practice of meditation without the cultivation of ethical safeguards can lead to self-deception, hallucination and even insanity. Therefore it is not a quick and easy passage into occult experiences that the aspirant should seek so much as a careful improvement of character.*

## CHAPTER V

### A TECHNIQUE OF SELF-ANALYSIS

SEATED comfortably in your chair or squatting tailor-fashion on a rug, breathing quietly and evenly, close your eyes and let your thoughts run over the question of what you really are.

You are about to begin your great adventure of self-inquiry.

One key to success in your practice is to think very slowly. The wheel of mind is to be slowed down, and consequently it will be unable to rush around from one thing to another, as it did formerly. Think slowly. Next formulate your words mentally with great care and precision. Choose and select each word accurately. Doing this will clarify your thought, for you cannot find a clear and definite phrase to fit it until you have done so.

First watch your own intellect in its working. Note how thoughts follow one another in endless sequence. Then try to realize that there is someone who thinks. Now ask: "Who is this Thinker?"

Who is this "I" that sleeps and wakes up; that thinks and feels; that works and speaks? What is it in us that we call the "I"?

Those who believe that matter is the only thing existing will tell you that it is the body; and that the sense of "I Am" arises within the brain at birth and disappears at the death or disintegration of the body.

Now in order to understand the real nature of this mysterious "I" and to find out its true relation to the functions of the body and brain we must make a penetrating analysis of personality, the apparent self.

This kind of self-knowledge does not mean merely sifting and cataloguing one's virtues, vices and qualities. It really means searching into one's essential spirit. To evoke the real man within you is to evoke your spiritual intelligence. When you can understand what lies behind the eyes which look at you every morning from the mirror, you will understand the mystery of life itself.

If you will but steadfastly regard the mystery that is in you, the divine mystery in man, it will eventually yield and display its secret. When a man begins to ask himself what he is, he has taken the first step upon a path which will end only when he has found an answer. For there is a permanent revelation in his heart, but he heeds it not. When a man begins to face his sub-mental mind and tries to strip the veil which covers it, persistent effort will provide its own reward.

The world is in a continual condition of flux, and man himself seems to be a mass of changing emotions and thoughts. But if he will take the trouble to make a deep analysis of himself, and to ponder calmly over it, he will eventually discover that there is a part of himself which receives the flow of impressions from the external world, and which receives the feelings and thoughts that arise therefrom. This deeper part is the true being of man, the unseen witness, the silent spectator, the Overself.

There is one thing which no man ever doubts. There is one belief to which every man always clings throughout the varied vicissitudes of life. And that is his own self-existence. He never stops for a moment to ask: "Do I exist?" He accepts it unfailingly.

I exist. That consciousness is real. Throughout life that remains ever. Of this we can be completely certain; but of its limitation to the fleshly frame we cannot be so certain. Let us, therefore, concentrate entirely upon this certainty—the reality of self-existence. Let us endeavour to locate it by confining our attention solely to the notion of self.

This, therefore, forms a good starting-point for our inquiry, since it is of such universal acceptance. The body changes; it gets feeble or strong, it remains sound or is injured. The mind changes; its outlook alters with time, its ideas are ever in flux. But the "I" consciousness persists from cradle to grave unchanged.

I am happy to-day, I am miserable to-morrow—these moods are but accidents or incidents in the continuity of the I. Moods of mind and heart change and pass, but through

them all the ego can name itself as that which remains unchanging amid the changing, spectator of the Passing Show
of this world. We are aware of all these things through the
"I," the self; without it all would be a total blankness. The
sense of "I am" cannot pass away. *Therefore, to know oneself is to find that point of consciousness from which observation of these changing moods may take place.* It is a
sad indication of how man has lost his centrality, his spiritual centre of gravity, that this point is usually wholly un-
noticed.

The "I" becomes the hapless victim of many different
desires and contrary thoughts until its spiritual integrity is
restored.

"A man commonly thinks that he knows what he means
by his self. He may be in doubt about other things, but
here he seems to be at home. He fancies that with the self
he at once comprehends both that it is and what it is. And
of course, the fact of one's own existence, in some sense,
is quite beyond doubt. But as to the sense in which this
existence is so certain, there the case is far otherwise,"
wrote F. H. Bradley, one of England's thinkers and philosophers.

§

An analysis of the constitution of man is thus the first
step. We begin by descending into ourselves. For at our
roots dwells the divine.

Whence comes this consciousness of "I"? It persists underneath all the changing moods of mind; it endures beyond every flux of feeling; it survives accident and con-
quers time. Does it arise out of our bodies?

No, that cannot be, for abnormal psychology and spiritualism conspire together to tell us that it *is* apart from
the flesh. The experiments of men like Sir Oliver Lodge
and Sir William Crookes and Professor William McDougall
and many other competent investigators into psychical research cannot be laughed away. We must look into them
and abide by the logical conclusion—however startling this
be—or else surrender our search for truth. We dare not
omit any data that put a fresh face on our theories. Whoever will look into the available records—and they are more

plentiful than would appear—can discover a sufficient number of cases to verify the truth of this assertion.

The connection between mind and body is so intimate that popular thought, whether learned or not, has readily accepted the *assumption* that the brain is mind, and body is self, yet it is only an assumption. It is possible that, *if self-consciousness can exist separately*, popular thought is mistaken and that the appearance is deceptive. This last thought we must consider, and consider without any bias either for or against the body.

§

A savage, low in the scale of evolution, has no other thought of "I" than the body and its desires. But a man more evolved, mentally developed, begins to refer to his body as "mine" because he has begun to feel that the intellect is no less a part of "I," and no less important a part than the body.

Certain psychologists and philosophers have persistently followed up the inquiry: "Is it possible for a human being to divorce his mind from his physical brain?" Such an inquiry obviously presupposes the likelihood that the brain is not necessarily the creator of thoughts, although superficially so; it might be the medium for their expression.

Nevertheless, our thinking is married to the brain which anatomists handle, but just as human marriages sometimes end in divorce, so is it possible for thought and flesh to end in temporary divorce also. Such a result has been brought about on set purpose by means of hypnotism in the West and by means of Yoga in the East. And in the researches of abnormal psychology and even spiritualism, there are evidences enough that the mind can have an existence of its own apart from the flesh.

It would be as sensible for me to attribute the power of thought to this body of mine, as it would be to attribute it to the ink in this pen. The body is inspired by one who acts no less than these written words are inspired by one who thinks. Yet people who are professedly intelligent, who would think twice and thrice before they would venture to attribute the qualities of mental creation and logical sense to ink, will not hesitate to bestow these qualities upon the

body which, being matter, is simply ink in another form!
The fact is that few people ever stop to consider this question of selfhood, and hence few people ever arrive at the
knowledge of its secret.

We cannot be body alone because, when a man's body
is completely stricken with paralysis, even his sight, touch,
hearing, taste and smell destroyed, he yet remains undimin-
ished as a self-conscious being. Strike off both his hands,
both his legs, take his eyes and parts of other organs—still
he does not feel less than himself, still the sense of "I" is
as strong as ever. Why should it not be possible that the
fleshly body is only a mass of matter which *I* move, *I* exercise, and *I* use—thus indicating that there is *someone*
who moves it, exercises it and uses it?

As your mind plays around the word *self*, accept for
consideration a strange idea. Your first response to this
thought may be an attempt to shake it off as being too
fantastic, but in the sequence you will be compelled to
consider it seriously, if you wish to get at its truth.

Here is the idea:

*If the body is the real self, then sleep could never su-
pervene nor death arrive.*

If the body is the real self, the awareness of one's existence would persist through every hour of the twenty-four.
Self is at the centre of consciousness and when sleep arrives
the self has withdrawn from the body, thus blanking out
awareness of the latter as one blanks out a scene when the
camera lens is covered. This unconsciousness of the body
during sleep is an indication that the self is merely a visitant in the house of flesh.

To say that in dreams we are retaining this awareness of
self whilst asleep is no refutal of this statement. Dream is
the bridge between the waking state and the deep sleep
state of complete unconsciousness. It represents the threshold
which must be crossed if one would penetrate into deep
sleep. This last stage is that which one must next consider
in order to arrive at a clearer notion of the self.

In the dreamless deep-sleep state I become absolutely
unconscious of the body—yet somehow "I" still exist. What
is that "I" doing, then, and where is it? When I fall into
a dreamless sleep, I forget the world entirely. Even the
keenest agony of the body is not strong enough to keep
me permanently awake; even the very thought "I" is for-

gotten. But self-existence, though temporarily blotted out, still persists in fact, for I awake later and remember my identity.

The American doctor Crile has produced some cases illustrating this principle, drawn from the abnormal conditions produced by the war. In one case he tells how an abandoned church was used as a temporary receiving station for soldiers suffering from terrible wounds. The doctor stole into the church at dead of night and found it perfectly silent. The men had had no sleep for five days and such was their extreme fatigue that not even their ghastly mutilations could keep them awake, and so all of them slept on *peacefully unaware of their bodies*. The incident, if it means anything at all, means that there is no self-consciousness in the body itself, *that the mental sense of selfhood can withdraw from the body*.

A hint that we cannot be body alone is thus found in the deep dreamless sleep state, when mind is plunged in unconsciousness; when the brain has stopped thinking and the created universe disappears from our view, and the actions of the physical body and sense-organs are apparently at a standstill, yet we emerge with the "I" notion again despite the seeming "near-death" of the body.[1] If self-consciousness in the body is due to the fact that self is but a visitant to it, then the disappearance of conscious being when we enter deep sleep is quite explicable. The sense of selfhood has withdrawn, we know not where, and left behind an insentient material form.

You have now been inquiring how to think of "I." You have been cutting a psychological cross-section through your own personality in the endeavour to reveal its true working. You have inquired whether the "I" is the body, and you could not *definitely* find it there. All that you could say with certainty is that it is being used by the self; that the self inheres in it alone you cannot trace with equal certainty.

[1] In the East there have been occasional authenticated cases of fakirs and Yogis who have hibernated like a frog for several days or weeks, with all the vital organs in a state of suspended animation, yet they have emerged from these death-like trances with a continuing sense of personality. In my previous book, *A Search in Secret India*, I have described a case which I personally observed, where a Yogi brought his heart to a complete cessation of function and even stopped all breathing—at will.

The sense of being yourself has remained. What is this sense? Can you grasp it?

No, you are forced to penetrate deeper than the body, and to explore the subtler realm of thoughts and feelings in your quest of the self.

Thus, using the scalpel of keen thought, prying into your inner self, you may arrive at the tentative position that the body is only part of your self and that the real essential source of the ego notion has so far not been traced out.

I have given the student only a rough outline of the kind of meditation he is to practise, and not every step of the long trail which he will need to follow upon the consideration of self, and it will be for him to develop these suggestive thoughts into more detail in his own way. It may take him but a few meditations to reach the point where he can accept these conclusions as probably correct, or it may take him a few months of practice. But until he can do so he cannot pass on to the second stage of this method. If his mind wanders away, if something arises to distract or disturb him, he should return undisheartened to his practice.

The driving determination of the illumined Will to bore its way through the solid mountain of thoughts and tendencies which we have erected around ourselves in the past, will one day receive a fit reward. When it emerges on the other side it becomes aware of that peace which passeth (intellectual) understanding.

Attention must be brought back again and again to this central theme; interest must be captured and held upon it. He must press on with this inner inquiry, moving from thought to thought in linked sequence.

Concentration is simply the power of controlling attention and of directing it towards one object. The light of the mind is vague and diffused in the average man; what we have to do is to concentrate it until it becomes a powerful searchlight; then upon whatever object we throw this powerful beam we shall be able to see it clearly and to acquire full knowledge about it. And this object may be merely material or it may be an abstract idea.

This is concentration—to take up one idea and to have neither time nor thought for anything else.

A piece of tissue paper might lie on the ground for all

time, but nothing exciting may happen to it; get a burning-glass and concentrate the sun's rays on one spot of that paper and something will soon happen.

You may have discovered, too, that the mind is like a restless monkey, but chain it to the post of a single object; tether it to the stake of one line of thought; then only will the monkey recognize you as its master, and be more ready to obey your orders.

Fix your mind firmly upon the subject of these reflections, brace it up to the necessary effort of will and concentration, and do not let disheartenment at apparent failure or slow progress deter you from continuing with the exercise. Thoughts of a totally irrelevant nature are sure to drift into your head in the middle of your practice; memories of recent events will form themselves before your mind's eye; pictures connected with personal associations are likely to intrude; desires, worries, work and what not will enter uninvited and try to hold the field of attention. But as soon as you become aware that the intrusion is out of place, dismiss it and begin at the point where you left off.

It is frequently the early stages of meditation that are the hardest, for then the mind is bombarded by discarded memories, drifting thoughts and emotional disturbances to an extent which surprises those who have never attempted the practice. The persistent and subconscious "pull" of the external world becomes apparent when we endeavour thus to recollect ourselves in meditation. We do not turn inwards by inclination. We cling to matter and tie ourselves up with the senses as naturally as a fish prefers the water.

Though man is one with the Higher Power which may be called God, the fact remains that he has lost the consciousness of this unity. And unless he makes the effort, as in regular meditations, frequent self-observation, or in true prayer, to detach himself increasingly from his external existence it is unlikely that he will recover this divine consciousness.

It is one of the hardest tasks we can undertake, this voluntary attempt to concentrate upon an abstract subject for fifteen to thirty minutes at a time, and to make man, so constantly extraverted, into a temporary introvert, but it is one of the most valuable. It will enable him to gaze upon the ethereal heights of pure thought. Such intellectual discipline may appear an intolerable labour to those who try it, but the reward is even better than the price we pay for it.

The average person is a puppet of environment and outside influences. He is governed by inherited tendencies and suggestions from other minds. To be able to control one's thoughts in the rush and stress of modern life is a valuable accomplishment, and this practice will bring that control.

We must dig with the drill of mind beneath the attraction of the physical world, and try to find the eternal reality which it hides. Then the secret of life, which has baffled the brilliant intellects of illustrious men, will be discovered and become our joyful possession.

§

The second stage of your inquiry into the true nature of self should be devoted to subjecting your emotional nature to critical analysis. You have tentatively repudiated the physical body as being the sum total of your "I" consciousness, and so you now turn to the next principal part of yourself.

Are you desire, doubt, hate, anger, like and dislike, passion, lust, hope, fear, or any of the other feelings which sway a man in changing sequence from time to time?

The argument which applies to the sleeping body applies equally to the sleeping emotions. When the latter are utterly quiescent and dead in dreamless sleep, the "I" notion still re-emerges upon waking after the apparent death of the emotions. And when, in the waking state, we sometimes experience moments of complete emotionlessness, the sense of personal being nevertheless remains. To transfer the earlier argument, if self-consciousness in the desires and emotions is due to the fact that self is but a visitant to them, then the disappearance of conscious being when we enter sound sleep is explicable. The sense of selfhood has withdrawn, we know not where, and left behind a collection of feelings which are born out of the attractions and repulsions of the sleeping body's sense-organs, or else out of the intellect.

This would also explain why the sense of selfhood remains unaffected by changes of experience. Feelings, desires and passions carry us hither and thither, but the self continuously exists. And it is perfectly possible for a man to retire from all experience of the outer world, and therefore from all the emotions which such experience brings with it, as in the conscious trance of the medieval Christian mystic or modern Indian Yogi, and yet retain a clear notion of selfhood. If self can divorce itself from emotion in this way and still continue its existence, then self and emotion are two different things and we cannot consider desires, fears, hates, sympathies or antipathies, and other emotional states as our real being.

Then again the fact that feelings change so largely, that you might like a person one week and dislike him the next, that the feelings of ten years ago may no longer represent you as you are to-day, indicates that they are transient in their essential nature, whereas the *sense* of "I" has remained unchanged through all those years.

Thus you arrive at the tentative position that neither emotion nor the body is your true self. When this point of view commends itself to you, the third stage may be entered. By this time you will have deepened your power of concentration; you will have begun, during the periods of practice, to remove your normal outward consciousness from sight, hearing and feeling into your interior, and to firmly concentrate your thoughts within yourself at such times.

The third stage is devoted to a consideration of the question: "Am I the thinking intellect?" Now the intellect usually receives its knowledge through the five senses, or from memory of such sense-channelled knowledge. The truth we expect to find within the domes of the average man's skull is therefore based on external experience.

I put forward what might seem to be an astounding proposition. Assuming that the intellect is not dependent on the flesh for its sole existence, I suggest that it is composed of nothing more than the endless sequence of thoughts, the endless series of ideas, concepts and memories, which normally make up the waking day, and that therefore there is no true selfhood even in the intellect. If all this aggregate of thoughts could be eliminated, then we should find that there is no such thing as a separate reasoning intellectual faculty. The intellect is but a name we give to a series of individual ideas.

This final proposition is more difficult to substantiate for it is rather a question to be decided by personal experience.

For I do not hesitate to say that if the intellect is but the continuous train of thoughts which pass and re-pass in procession through the brain, then, under certain conditions man may cease to think and yet remain clearly conscious of himself. This has occurred several times and the history of mysticism, both Oriental and European, attests the fact.

Every argument which was applied to the denial of emotion as the true self can now be applied to the denial of intellect. Think—and you will realize that it must be so.

Intellect is that which thinks *within* ourselves. It is not our self and this is indicated by the fact that during thinking we feel vaguely that something in us is quietly watching these thoughts.

The fact that some insane people lose their intellect, and that it is sometimes restored to them, is another indication that it is a property which can be taken away from, or restored to, *a possessor*.

This was the celebrated attitude of Descartes. He maintained that the mere act of thinking involved the existence of a Thinker, of the one who carries on this reflective activity. "*Je pense, donc je suis* (I think, therefore I am)," was his famous philosophical proposition. It was a tremendous claim and found its powerful opponents. And its logical result was that Descartes was compelled to infer that this Thinker, this "I," was intrinsically immaterial and therefore independent enough to have its own existence apart from the fleshly body with which it is nevertheless so intimately bonded. Thus though Descartes never brought his account of the self to the farther which I propose doing, he made a good point beginning.

Further, the moods of thought are in a constant process of change. You may believe in one opinion to-day and hold its contrary on the morrow. How can you seize on any set of thoughts and say: "This represents my self," when next year it may misrepresent you? Yet the sense of being yourself, of I, has remained, whereas your outlook might greatly change.

Again, when you have been quietly contemplating some matter you feel that *something in you* is watching the thoughts, something which accepts some of them and rejects others. Who is it that thinks? The very fact that you pick and choose among these thoughts indicates that there is a separate unit which uses the brain's mechanism. That "something in you"—is it the self? Hitherto you have been so absorbed and so occupied with your egoistic thoughts, your personal feelings and physical activities that you have not tried to pin consciousness down to this inner "something." You have not tried to detach yourself from thought, feeling or action for even a moment; therefore you have never been able to study the nature of whatever it is that lives within this house of flesh.

If we could track down, as we can by this practice, this "something in us," we would find it to be our true self. It is always there, but the press of our thoughts and the continual attention given to external objects through the senses, cries down its gentle presence. Thinking is a power which may bind us or set us free. The average man unconsciously uses it for the former purpose; the practitioner of this way of self-inquiry consciously uses it to gain freedom.

The unstopping wheels of our brain whir endlessly on in revolutions of petty or important thoughts, and whether they deal with merely trivial matters or with noble and high subjects, it does not seem that we can stop their movement. Perhaps the intellect is only a machine for thinking, rendering its account to logic in a purely mechanical manner.

Thoughts surge up ceaselessly and disturb the primal repose of the mind. So long continued has this process become, in the history of man, that we have come to regard it as our normal state. To draw the mind back into a calm rest, much more so to be without thoughts, we regard as an abnormal condition. We have taken a tradition for a truth and it would be well to inquire how far these values of ours are justified.

Thus far we have discovered that the limits hitherto set by ourselves on the notion of "self" are fictitious, that "thoughts" which in their totality constitute the intellect, need not be the psychic barrier which hems us in.

By this introspective analysis we have subjected our own being to critical examination, and taken in turn each principal part of it, endeavouring to discover whether it is the essential self we are seeking, the foundation of the notion "I."

We have penetrated our inner being, and thus learnt that the outer world, which is revealed to us by our senses, need not be the only condition of our conscious existence.

One result of this meditation is that it will eventually

enable you to watch how the intellectual, emotional and bodily machine works in reference to your self, to get you outside of your personal self. There is no danger of becoming ultra-introspective through this exercise, because it renders you more impersonal instead of emphasizing the personality. It draws you away from purely personal moods into utterly impersonal ones.

But we have yet to track down the soul. Now I do not care overmuch for that word "soul," since it carries different meanings to different people. It has served a high use with some lofty spirits of our race, but it has also been tortured into submission by narrow deluded minds and narrow deluding religionists. I would fain leave it out of my lines if I could, but I cannot. It comes bearing the grey burden of troublesome theologies, with which a rationalist such as I am would prefer to have nothing to do. But the word "self" covers all that I mean with a completeness and adequacy that the feebler word does not. The early Hindus understood this so well that their word for "self" is exactly similar to their word for "soul." Self is a collection of personal experiences; it includes all physical, mental and emotional experiences which string themselves like pearls upon this thread of "I," yet it merges itself within that vast impersonal and divine being which constitutes the true limitless glory of man.

One encounters the profoundest difficulties in attempting to make these subtle matters perfectly comprehensible to the ordinary intelligence without indulging in abstruse and abstract metaphysics, but I have made the effort because I know that whoever will patiently ponder over these thoughts in the right prejudiceless spirit will eventually be rewarded by a faint inner recognition of their truth, and by a faint intuitive understanding of their significance. It will then be for him to follow up this clue by means of the threefold practice outlined in this book.

## CHAPTER VI

### A BREATHING EXERCISE TO CONTROL THOUGHTS

THE student who has completed the third stage of the meditation outlined in the foregoing chapter, reveals thereby that he has set his hand to the plough with dogged patience and earnest endeavour. He has undertaken a task which calls for some of the best qualities in man's character, and for some of the most unused mental capacities. His effort is indeed praiseworthy because it has to be carried on alone, in the solitude of his own room, and he has none of the gregarious comfort which class study offers to the pupils of subjects other than self-knowledge. The line of reflection laid down for him in these pages is precisely that line which is best suited to solitary meditation. Were he fortunate enough to be in close association with an Adept who could demonstrate in himself the rare attainment which he seeks, then indeed it is quite probable that the labour of such interrogative meditation would become far less, for such a Teacher intentionally kindles through mere personal contact alone the fire of spiritual experience in those who combine aspiration towards it with faith in him; such a Teacher will give more in a few meetings to a worthy pupil than the latter can gain by many months of solitary plodding.

But a genuine Adept is exceedingly hard to find in the modern world, though his feeble imitators are not lacking, and so these pages are penned to give a little help for the student who depends on self-effort alone. If he will read these pages with close keen attention, heartfelt interest and a genuine desire to discover truth at the cost of parting with personal prejudices; if he will absorb their content in such a way that the mere perusal of the book provides him with an inner experience, then he will travel far and achieve an attractive spiritual reward for his trouble.

If these pages are read in the right manner, with profound attention and deep feeling, they may awaken secret forces which are latent in the being of man and then the reading will itself provide the student with a genuine spiritual experience. For it not only pictures a path to the divine self, but may enable the sincere student to travel along this path.

The close of this third stage closes also the preparatory period of the student's inner journey. Hitherto he has worked hard at his practices, but without much tangible reward; henceforth he will enter upon a course whereon he will gain new experiences which will amply compensate him for every minute of effort and which foreshadow the splendid goal that ultimately awaits him. All doubt will gradually begin to disappear, all uncertainty will gradually fall away from him who has found the right path to true self-knowledge.

So far we have probed into the mysterious recesses of self, we have penetrated part of the way by the aid of the faculty of thought, but we cannot arrive at the quintessential nature of the self by its aid alone. We may now perceive how man is crushed against the barriers of mystery as soon as he begins to think really deeply. Where thinking cannot go, something else is to arise and lead us on. Rational thought provides us with a splendid instrument wherewith to comprehend life and the world up to a point, but it is a mistake to imagine that it is therefore the only instrument available to us.

That new element is intuition, immediate understanding. When thinking fails we may find this state of intuitive guidance by delicate and careful search. It is there, within us, and it is open for all to discover. This is the meaning of Jesus' phrase: "Search, and ye shall find." Few ever take the trouble to search inwardly in this way and, therefore, few find.

How is the intuition to be awakened?

When the reasoning, thinking intellect subsides its activity, the intuition has a clear field in which to manifest itself. When the waves of thought no longer rise and fall upon the surface of the mind, the latter becomes like a calm pellucid pool in which the sun of intuition can reflect itself without difficulty and without distortion. It is therefore necessary to find some means to reduce the constant agitation of the intellect.

That can be done by a twofold process. The first consists of an effort to direct thoughts along a single channel of a certain kind, i.e. concentration upon an exalted abstract idea. If you have faithfully practised the meditation-exercise already given, or deliberately yielded yourself up to inspired works of art, then this part of the process will to some extent have inevitably been done and intuitive minutes will be known.

The second process entails the control of breathing. The reason is there exists a profound connection between breath and thought. The movements of breath beat time, in a most remarkable fashion, with the movements of thought. Breathing seems quite a simple act and it may appear strange why it should have any effect upon mental action at all, but investigation and experiment indisputably prove the fact. Most people undervalue the powers of the breath, but the early Jesuits in the West and the early Yogis in India knew better, for they embodied breathing exercises in their system of training. Those who have not studied the subject cannot realize what striking changes can be brought about in the body and the mind through the simple means of changing the breath rhythm.

A child understands that a breath quickly blown into hot milk will cool it, and that the same breath blown into cold hands will warm them. But we have yet to understand that breath can also be used to resist the diseases of the body, to endure the effects of extreme heat and cold, and to change the tone of one's thoughts. Consider for a moment that when you are excited, your breath comes in quick gasps, but when you are plunged in deep thought, it comes quietly and slowly. Watch a man who breathes in tumultuous jerks and you will see that his nerves are equally restless. Does this not show how much friendship there is between breathing and the mind?

Breathing is normally an unconscious function of life. Any attempt to change it will at once turn it into a conscious function. And so the student who wishes to affect his mentality through the breath must set aside brief periods when he deliberately alters its rhythm. If these periods are utilized in the manner to be described, carefully following the simple instructions which follow, the resultant effect upon his thoughts will in time be most marked. But it is important that these instructions are not departed from or varied in any way.

Here a word of warning against the indiscriminate practice of published Indian Yoga breathings is essential. With a teacher to guide and to protect, the path of Yoga breath control is rendered safe, but without one it is a path of great danger. As an Indian Yogi adept once told me while we sat together in a shady grove: "The ancient masters who knew the different effects of different breathings tell us that through the breath we may make ourselves as powerful as gods equally as we may go down into insanity, incurable diseases and sudden death. You will then understand that where the rewards are so much greater, the dangers are no less great. In our system there are exercises for different purposes and if some are almost harmless, others if wrongly done are potent for grave injury."

The breathing exercise which is given here, however, is a safe one and may be practised without fear. It is the only Yoga exercise of this kind which may safely be practised without the supervision of a teacher, while it is so simple that no one can fail to do it rightly. But persons who suffer with heart disease should never practise any form of breathing exercise whatever.

§

The exercise consists in slowing down the rhythm of breathing to a point below the normal rate. The precise point cannot be prescribed here as it varies with different persons, partly according to varying lung capacities and partly according to different degrees of nervous sensibility. The average healthy person breathes approximately fifteen times each minute. Nevertheless, the full reduction should not be made straightway. It is always better to introduce such changes gradually and not violently.

Begin by exhaling very slowly, then inhale gently, then hold the breath momentarily, then breath out again. Practise this with full attention and with eyes closed. It is important that the student should pour all his consciousness into his breathing until he seems to live in it for the time being.

This exercise is to be practised by beginners for five minutes—*no longer*. Advanced students may extend the time successively to ten, fifteen and twenty minutes as they progress. None should go beyond the last time-limit.

A slow, regular and quiet effort alone is called for; there should be no straining and no violent deep breathing as that would defeat the student's aim; and complete muscular relaxation should reign. He may take it as a sign of success when the breath rhythm flows gently and effortlessly, so that if a feather were held before the nostrils it would not move. Yet if he feels the slightest discomfort or gasping for breath at any moment, he should stop at once and realize that he is practising wrongly.

Breathe through *both* nostrils: any European or American student who practises the alternate nostril Yoga breathing is taking great risks with his health and sanity; leave it alone. Dilated lungs are the least danger. Such artificial and unnatural breathing exercises are usually practised with a view to obtaining psychic powers: they have nothing in common with the natural control of breathing here advocated as a means of quietening the restless fever of thought and making the respiration as peaceful as that of a babe in the womb.

This exercise is based on the simple fact that breathing is a medium between the mind and the body, because it supplies arterialized blood to the brain. To diminish the cycle of breaths is to curtail the supply of blood to the brain, and therefore to retard the cycle of thoughts. "Breath is the horse and mind is the rider," say the Tibetans. Thus the tension and relaxation of the brain, the uprising and disappearance of thoughts, correspond in peculiar harmony with the cycle of breathing and can be brought under control.

The effect upon the student of consciously dropping the rhythm of his breathing will be a pleasant relaxed mood, a calming of the constant vibration of thought, a pouring of oil upon the troubled sea of life, and a more abstracted mental condition. And the intent concentration of his attention will cause him to forget other things in the act itself, so that he feels that he has become a "breath-being," as it were. He steeps himself utterly in the changed breathing process, blends his mind with it, submerges all other thoughts into watching it, and so be-

comes temporarily transformed into a subtler, more sensitive
person. Such a stage is not reached immediately, but follows after weeks of regular practice.

The power of this single exercise over the mind can
scarcely be appreciated by those who have never practised
it. It restores a harmonious rhythm to the human machine.
It can transform an agonized heart into a heart at peace
with the world.

Some years ago a well-known Fleet Street journalist was
unexpectedly promoted to the editorship of a famous
London Sunday newspaper. He was Scotch and naturally
ambitious, so he resolved to more than "make good" in his
new post. He spared himself no effort, but drove himself
like a slave-driver to make a success of his editorship. He
worked so hard, undertook so much responsibility, that a
time came when outraged Nature demanded her inexorable
price. He collapsed and was carried away from his office
and from his post a nervous wreck.

For several months he lay in a seaside nursing home
slowly rebuilding his shattered nerves and worn-out body.
But it was not until he was given this breathing exercise,
that he quickened his recovery and returned to Fleet Street,
not merely a well man but a new man. For his entire outlook on life had changed through practising this simple
breathing exercise. Henceforth he was able to see deeper
into life, to grasp the spiritual purpose behind things and
to sense the divine harmony underneath all the discords
of modern existence.

This exercise may also be used at other times during the
day quite apart from its present purpose. If, at any time,
your self-control is threatened by violent passions or dis-
turbing emotions, of whatever kind, immediately resort to
the practice of this breathing exercise until the danger has
passed. Its effectiveness under such conditions will be found
quite remarkable.

For the purposes of this self-inquiry, however, this breath-
control is only to be practised by the student immediately
after the meditation-exercise has ended. He will have arrived
at an apparent cul-de-sac in the final point of his meditation,
at what seems to be a mental blank wall. For, having in-
terrogated the body, the feelings and the intellect in their
turn, he will have failed to find in each of them the elusive
"self" which he seeks. He will be faced with nothingness,

for what exists in a man after these three have been eliminated? With that he finishes his meditation, ends the racking of his brain by unfamiliar introspections and turns his mind to the above breath-control exercise.

When he succeeds with this practice, he will begin to gain a mental state in which thoughts lie stilled like charmed serpents. He will begin to gain the placidity of mind which is one of the chief aims of Indian Yoga, but he will obtain it without having to endure the strain, struggle and danger involved in the Yoga breathing exercises which unwise persons have indiscriminately made known to the West.

## CHAPTER VII

### THE AWAKENING TO INTUITION

WHEN the student has finished his breathing exercise he is ready for the next stage of this practice, the next effort which he is asked to put forth. If he has practised this exercise properly and with success, he will catch the mind like a bird in a net, its constant flight stopped, its restless activity quiet, so that it lies within the net of breath-control without a flutter of its wings. He should not attempt to revert back to normal breathing by means of an effort, rather should he let his breathing process adjust itself naturally. His mind is now to be withdrawn from concentrating upon the breath and turned away towards the next step—the awakening to intuition. I say *to* intuition advisedly, because the latter is always present, unsleeping, and needs no awakening.

He begins by reverting to the questioning and searching attitude which he adopted during the meditation, but this time his interrogation is addressed, not to the body, desires or thoughts, but to the mysterious darkness which environs his mind.

*Who Am I?*
*Who is this being that dwells within this body?*

Let him address these silent questions to himself, slowly, intently, and with utter concentration of soul.

Then let him wait for a few minutes, meditating quietly and without effort upon these questions.

Thereafter, let him make a silent humble request, a half-prayer if he wishes, directed to the Overself in the very centre of his being, to reveal its existence to him. The words in which he formulates this request may be his own, but they should be simple, brief and direct. Let him ask as though he were addressing an intimate friend and a true one. "Ask and it shall be given unto you," was the direction of Jesus, whose consciousness was purely that of the Overself, to his hearers.

Having made the request or silently uttered the prayer let him pause and wait expectantly, even confidently, for a response. I say "confidently" yet withal there should be a profound humility in his soul when he is asking for the divine revelation to come to him. Humility is the first step on the secret path—and it will also be the last. For before the divinity can begin to teach him through its own self-revelation he must first become teachable, i.e. humble.

Intellectual ability and learning are admirable things and adorn a man, but intellectual pride puts up a strong barrier between him and that higher life which is ever calling to him, albeit silently. The intellectually proud sit upon their puny pedestals and wait to be worshipped, when all the while there is a deity dwelling in the deeps of their hearts who is alone worthy to receive worship. The intellectual self seeks to strut like a proud peacock before the admiring gaze of the world; but the true begetter of its talents and creator of our achievements, the one who permeates it with the principle of life and thus permits it to exist, is quite content to remain in the background, unknown and un-noticed by men.

It is the hardest of tasks to abase oneself to a realization of one's own littleness, ignorance and vanity. Yet it is the greatest of attainments for it leads directly to that finding of the divine life which Christ promised to all who would lose the personal life.

We do not need the knowledge and culture of a distinguished mind to understand and appreciate these teach-ings. The simple and untutored and the primitive can as readily enter into them by an act of faith and prayer, and can more easily enter into the mood of reverence.

When we approach the Overself by the path of self-inquiry, the matured studies of the philosopher avail him little over the man in the street. This is not because such studies are valueless; on the contrary they train the mind in useful habits of abstraction, concentration and depth. It is because they engender a pride of learning and an egotism of self-importance which erect gates across the true path. The mastery of a dozen different systems of intricate philosophy is not a task for the many; yet the mastery of personal pride is infinitely harder. Humility comes more easily to the illiterate and ignorant, because they are conscious of their mental and social inferiority. And humility is essential at every stage of the Secret Path.

The great elemental secrets of life are so simple that few see them. People are complicated, intellects are complicated, not life. Therefore I say: Treasure in your heart and carry in your mind the memorable saying of Jesus that "Except ye become as a little child ye shall not enter the kingdom of heaven." Tremendous teleological speculations are not necessary to understand the simple truths of the Spirit.

Hitherto all the student's efforts at finding the true self have been positively directed, personally willed, conscious and voluntary. He is now almost at the point where there should be a complete reversal of procedure, where the personality must cease making any further efforts because it has reached the end of its tether.

The whole process of meditation is simply to select this one higher topic of self-inquiry out of the multitude of ideas, to think firmly upon that alone and of nothing else. Then, when the attitude and quality of concentration are thus strongly developed, the student drops even this special line of thinking, withdraws inward and questions who it is that is thinking. He does not endeavour to obtain an answer by thinking *about* the Thinker; he begins to let all thoughts drop away and to fasten his full attention *upon becoming aware* of this being who has been covered over by the screen of never-ending thoughts.

During this pause which follows his silent request, he should suspend his thoughts so far as he can by adopting an attitude of "listening-in" for a response. After waiting for two or three minutes, he may repeat his request and then pause again. After the second waiting period of three or four minutes, he may repeat it for a third and final time. Then he should wait patiently, expectantly, for a period of about five minutes, his body still, his breathing slow and quiet, his mind becalmed. This ends his meditation.

The key to a correct understanding of this stage is in remembering that it is the subconscious reaction to your conscious effort which is now all-important. The conscious practice of mental quiet has been useful in sharpening attention; it is like ringing a door-bell, now you must wait for the subconscious to make its appearance. Do not overstrain, do not overdo; give the Overself some credit for intelligence of its own, for action of its own.

You may pass through a period when no response comes, when empty nothingness alone reigns supreme within your soul. Before you leave this "no man's land" of the soul a feeling of intense loneliness may overcome you. Nevertheless it will eventually pass away. If you are not prepared to exercise patience while working silently for this revelation you defeat any possibility of success.

Patience is important. We must wait humbly for the revelation of the Infinity which is within man. Until that sacred hour we are poor orphans. Those who introduce any element of impatience into their period of mental quiet, are merely handicapping themselves.

Henceforth the student must watch carefully for the first confirmatory signs and tokens that he is upon the right way, the first faint evidences of the stirrings of his deeper self within him. Such signs and tokens are shown us by the soul, but they are often misunderstood or simply not noticed.

They come quietly, as quietly as the sun steals into a darkened world, so quietly that he is likely to dismiss them as useless fantasies, meaningless thoughts or unimportant imaginings. This would be a great error. The Overself's voice is first heard like a soft breath, and he must pay full heed to it. The gentlest stirrings within the heart must receive his full and undivided attention, and he must look upon them with respect and veneration as ambassadors from a higher realm. For these quiet monitors are but heralds of a dynamic force which is yet to come and which will transfuse and interpenetrate his body with heavenly power.

There are certain subtle tones of feeling, delicate shades of thought, which are usually unnoticed, overlooked or dismissed in ordinary daily life. These disregarded experiences are the very things the meditator must seize upon for culture and development. He will focus all his power of attention on them whenever they appear, striving to yield himself up to them utterly.

In such strange moments he discovers what is almost a second self within. These moments may be rare; he may not even get them except at irregular intervals; but their existence evidences something that is. These ecstatic moments provide a clue to the true nature of man.

Within every single one of us lies well upon well of spiritual peace untapped, of spiritual intelligence untouched. From time to time whispers come to us from this second self, whispers that urge us on to practise self-control, to take the higher path and to transcend selfishness. We must heed those whispers and exploit those rare moments. They give us glimpses of what we may become. If these moments when this spiritual perception flashes across us could be extended, happiness eternal would be ours. For there *is* something which occasionally makes itself felt in this manner in the mysterious depth of the soul. What it is we hardly know, but what it says we may know. "All that is best in thee, THAT am I," is its silent voice. It is one with us, yet sainted and set apart.

The object of this work in mental quiet is to enter into a realm which psychologists often denominate as the unconscious.

The response of awakening intuition may come the first time this exercise is practised, or it may not come until after several weeks or even months of daily practice. The student who has completely mastered all the earlier stages is now in a position to benefit markedly by the help of a *genuine* Adept, who can now rapidly bring the intuition to birth for him by certain secret methods. If such a meeting is impossible or impracticable, because the finding of genuine Adepts is exceedingly difficult in the modern world, then he must continue to adhere faithfully to the instructions given here.

§

You may considerably assist your development at this stage by beginning to watch yourself at odd times during the day. You may stop yourself, almost unexpectedly, and observe what you are doing, feeling, saying or thinking, letting your self-observation be made in a detached, impartial and impersonal spirit.

"*Who* is doing this?"
"*Who* is feeling this emotion?"
"*Who* is speaking these words?"
"*Who* is thinking these thoughts?"

Put such silent questions to yourself as often as you wish, but put them abruptly, suddenly, and then wait expectantly, quietly, for some intuitive inner response. So far as you can, drop all thoughts during this pause. Such introspective inquiry need not occupy you more than a minute or two at odd times. The placid breathing may profitably be induced in conjunction with this exercise in self-observation and self-inquiry.

In this manner you will begin to break up the complacent attitude which accepts the personal self's body-based outlook, and to free yourself from the illusion that the outer person is the complete being of man. The practice of suddenly observing oneself, one's desires, moods and actions, is especially valuable because it tends to separate the thoughts and desires from the sense of selfhood which normally inheres in them, and thus tends to keep consciousness from being everlastingly drowned in the sea of the five physical senses. Furthermore, it will reinforce in a helpful manner the work which is being done to penetrate the so-called unconscious during the periods of mental quiet. Indeed, it might be said that the three practices, self-observation, daily quiet and placid breathing, are complementary. All aim at overcoming the tendencies towards complete self-identification with the body, the desires and the intellect which are to-day regarded as normal and natural.

The human race has yielded to such tendencies since time immemorial, and thus the common identification of self with body has arisen. The cure lies in gradually erasing these tendencies by repeated quest of the true self, the

Overself, in times of mental quiet, and by constant self-observation at odd times during the day. No matter how deeply fixed in oneself these tendencies are, they can gradually be smoothed away by means of these practices.

The intellect which is repeatedly turned inwards upon this inquiry, yields in time to habit and automatically begins to present our changing emotions, desires, thoughts and actions to us in the light of the Overself, i.e. as things which are being experienced within ourselves but are merely mechanical responses to external stimuli.

One inevitable result of all these practices will be that your attitude towards things, people and events will gradually change. You will begin to express the qualities which are natural to the Overself, the qualities of noble outlook, perfect justice, the treatment of one's neighbour as oneself.

Turn your mind repeatedly to THAT which is the silent spectator within yourself, and fix it there. This inward-turning is a mental process, an intellectual activity based on an attitude of self-inquiry, but in the stage which follows there is a yielding up of all thoughts to the intuitive feeling which arises from within and which leads one's awareness to the Innermost.

You have always been exercising your intellect and emotions, rarely your intuition; henceforth you must begin to change this by bringing your intuitive feeling out of latency as often as possible. It will take time, this search after the right intuition amid the medley of feelings and thoughts which normally compose our inner selves, but persistent inquiry will find it out.

There is no moment of the day when you may not profitably divert the current of thought and seek within yourself to ascertain the Overself. You must begin to ride the horse of mind and drive it in an inward direction. You will begin this quest in the ordinary state of spiritual darkness, in the ordinary condition of self-oblivion, the victim of mechanically-aroused desires and repulsions. But if you continue with these practices you will gradually feel your way inwards to greater freedom.

There is no happiness for the man who is not free. Whether a king imprisoned by his duties in his palace, or a convict tied to a prison-cell, it is a truism that the soul loves freedom. Here we have a clue to the nature of true happiness. Eternal and unchanging liberty must be a part

of its nature, and a liberty of this rare kind can be found
nowhere else except in the Overself.

One proceeds thus by imperceptible degrees to follow
thought back into its unseen home. So long as you are in
bondage to thinking, so long does intuition lie beyond your
reach.

Follow the way of constant self-inquiry and you will
make even thinking serve you as a means to freedom, and
the very questions you put yourself will be stepping-stones
to the questionless state of the Overself.

You will better understand the *rationale* of the threefold
practice—mental quiet, placid breathing and self-observation—by studying the following picture of man's relation
to his Overself.

We may say that the person exists by virtue of, through
the life force of, and by permission of the Overself. The
thoughts and desires and resulting actions of a person are
normally almost entirely occupied with things belonging to
the external world. We may picture the personal self sitting
inside man's body and constantly engaged in viewing the
world around through the doorway of the five physical
sense-organs. The result of this preoccupation with outside
objects is that it is constantly attracted or repelled, as the
case may be, busily thinking, desiring, or setting the body
to action, *until it has entirely forgotten its place of birth,*
which is the Overself. Thus it has fallen into the ironical
position of a being which has not only lost all memory of
its Father, but actually denies all possibility of the very
existence of that Father.

THAT out of which thoughts arise is the true being of
man, the true self. There is an unknown and unnoticed gap
between every two thoughts, between every two breaths,
wherein man pauses momentarily for the flimsiest fraction
of a second. During that pause, which flashes by with
such immeasurable rapidity, he returns to his primal self
and rests anew in his real being. If this were not so, if
this did not happen thousands of times every day, man
could not continue to exist and his body would fall dead
to the ground, an insentient piece of matter. For the Overself is the hidden source of his life; its force sustains and
maintains him; and these constant returns to it enable man
to "pick up" the life-power which he needs for living, for
thinking and for feeling. These tiny fragments of time are

experienced by everyone but recognized at their true worth by few. THAT *is* eternally, but you, the personal self, exist, "come out of" it for a time only.

§

Fixing your attention upon the question, "Who am I," and attempting to pursue its solution with all the ardour you can command, a time will come one day, during your half-hour practice of mental quiet, when you shall be so deeply engrossed in this effort as to be largely unmindful of what is around you. This condition of intense reverie provides you with the appropriate state wherein the great event of self-revelation can take place.

As a matter of fact to obtain access to one's own soul is not such a rare feat as it may seem. Many prepare the appropriate conditions for it unawares. The artist, when he abstracts his mind from external surroundings in the rapt absorption of his art, does it. He touches ecstasy in a minor measure, forgets himself in his work or vision. It is in this state that geniuses have achieved their finest creations, their best work.

"When I am, as it were, completely myself, entirely alone, and of good cheer: it is on such occasions that my ideas flow best and most abundantly, whence and how they come I know not, nor can I force them," Mozart confessed to a friend.

The writer lost in reverie over his theme, his mind sunk so deeply in a single train of ideas that he fails to recognize things, persons or events that are about him; the painter so profoundly absorbed in contemplating the picture he is making that he is oblivious of the hours; and above all the musician rapt in the ardour of musical composition, all these are unconsciously practising meditation! But you, who follow the path of self-inquiry, are to do it *consciously*.

When Leonardo da Vinci was at a loss for creative ideas, he would look into a heap of ashes and the concentration involved would usually succeed in developing a reverie wherein the ideas he needed were born.

"A kind of waking trance I have frequently had quite from boyhood, when I have been all alone," wrote England's Poet Laureate, Lord Tennyson, in a letter to a friend.

"Out of the intensity of the consciousness of the individuality, the individuality itself seemed to dissolve and fade away into boundless being; and this not a confused state, but the clearest of the clear, the surest of the sure; utterly beyond words; where death was an almost laughable impossibility, the loss of personality (if so it were) seeming no extinction but the only true life."

Tennyson expressed a similar idea in a beautiful verse:

"If thou would'st hear the Nameless, and wilt dive
Into the Temple-cave of thine own self,
There, brooding by the central altar, thou
May'st haply learn the Nameless hath a voice,
By which thou wilt abide, if thou be wise."

Sir Isaac Newton, late one morning, was found sitting half-dressed in bed, sunk in meditation, and on another occasion remained for a long time in his cellar, where a train of thought had taken possession of him while in the act of fetching a bottle of wine for his guests.

Lord Kitchener had moods of "brown studies" wherein his eyes turned up on their axes, as though gazing at the root of his nose. He would then appear quite unaware of what was going on around him. He emerged from these moods in a condition of inspired understanding.

As concentration deepens, the external world is slowly forgotten. The mental chambers become empty of every thought save this dominant expectancy of a response from the inner Self. It is a species of self-hypnotism if you like, but it "works," and its value is to be judged by its result.

At this stage you will cease all striving, you will not try to achieve anything, but rather allow something to be achieved in you; you will let go of the arguing intellect and yield to faith, to holy expectancy, to sublime trust. For henceforth whatever will be done is to be done by divine action, and not your own. You question things no longer, but submit, questionless, to that which is to appeal to your inmost being. Allow this inner being to take possession of you, to take control of you. We instinctively waver and recoil from that mysterious state wherein the senses are almost suspended, but do not fear.

Thoughts no longer leap through the mind, but die down into a slow procession as the meditative mood deepens.

"Silence is God," says a French writer. Yes, but silence

of body, of thoughts, of desires—not merely aural silence. In this sublime moment God is beginning to take possession of your soul; all you have to do is to practice the utmost self-surrender.

To sit in this listening quietude, following the thread of intuition, is a strange experience. The world-machine seems to slow down; and within this point that is yourself, the Absolute begins to emerge. This is the mysterious and momentous hour when the mind first breaks out of its self-created chrysalis. The response to your silent invocation comes at first in the form of a faint and, at first, impalpable intuition, an *in-leading*. Guided by the Ariadne-thread of awakened *intuition*, you are being brought to your own native hearth. Or it may first take shape as a message which will be impressed upon your mind in vivid words. In that case you will then find a strange temple within yourself—a temple wherein you will be both preacher and hearer. A mysterious condition gradually arises wherein one becomes strangely aware of this "otherness." It is as if one part of your nature watches what the other part does. He that finds this sacred unseen threshold is indeed fortunate for—"few there be that find it."—Yet they are the few who know that man's best and highest wishes fall short indeed of the treasure he is yet to attain. Or the vision of a shining symbolic picture may pattern itself before your mind's eye. You may see a cross with a circle standing out in glorious colours, or a radiant five-pointed star. Or you may experience nothing more than a melting tenderness in the heart, a gentle sensation of sinking inward into a beautiful rest.

Those who spend the years soliciting some intimation or revelation from the august guest within, will with time receive a rich reward. A single glimpse of that mysterious stranger takes the troubles out of our life and puts them under our feet. One hallowed word from his oracular lips bestows a bliss which melts our smaller self in cosmical joy.

The great De Beer diamond fields of South Africa were discovered through a child picking out of the wall of an old Dutch farm a small coloured pebble—out of a wall which, for years and years, had been passed and re-passed many thousands of times by people blind to the treasure at their elbows. How many people have heard the gentle whisper of the inner self or felt its faint guidance, only to brush the visitants aside without understanding; how many have dismissed as mere thoughts the early intimations of diviner life? For this magnetic centre deeply buried in the flesh of man which constitutes his real essential nature, which is the father of all his finer deeds, sometimes reveals its presence in nothing more tangible than such delicate monitions.

The greatest truths sometimes come unheralded into the mind. We know only that yesterday we could not accept them, but to-day we hold them gladly. So it is with a man when the first rays from the sun of immortality begin to fall upon him.

You will find, if you yield yourself still further to these sensations, that you will be less inclined to billow the mind with waves of thought, that you will silently give them the command to be still. Thoughts will come and go with increasing slowness. Do not hesitate to let all thinking stop, if you can. But this represents a point which is highly advanced, a point which one must not strive for as in that case only an artificial blankness will ensue. It must and does come of its own accord through the inner workings of the "subconscious" spiritual self.

The stoppage of thought is not necessarily a means of attaining the consciousness of our divine self; if that were so, epileptics would have the spiritual power of a Christ and lunatics would possess the wisdom of a Buddha. But what is true is that we have covered over our divine nature with thoughts and desires; therefore we must proceed to uncover it if we would know it. Hence the difference—and a very vital one—between the lunatic who stares with glassy eyes into vacancy, and the mystic who stares with shining eyes into seeming vacancy, is the difference between one who has lost the power to think but has not attained to the knowledge of the inner self, and one who has conquered the tyranny of thought and can suspend its action at will, while consciously being aware of his true spiritual self.

Thinking as we ordinarily know it is a heavy veil flung over the beautiful face of the divinity within us. Raise the veil a little by letting the mind come to rest as a ship glides into harbour and then is still, and you will perceive somewhat of a beauty you can never forget.

Is the conscious cessation of thought really possible? The

best answer to this question is an appeal to direct experience. Men who have explored the mind's depths have ultimately reached a point where they have been compelled to stop their search, for their thought has been held in a state of suspension. For the mind may be likened to a wheel in constant motion, and thought is simply the automatic result of this motion. When the wheel is brought to a dead end, all thinking is sure to cease.

Many inexperienced people will object that to stop thinking is to stop consciousness. The actual experience of the process reveals that this is not so, that a new and extremely vivid awareness heightens our normal consciousness. We need to differentiate pure consciousness from the faculty of thinking.

Death is the secret of life. We must empty ourselves if we would be filled. When the mind has poured out all its thoughts, a vacuum is created. But this can last only for a few seconds. Then a mysterious influx of divine life will enter. This is the descent of the Holy Ghost.

It is in this state of conscious cessation of thought that the truth of one's self, heretofore hidden from us by activity, desires and thoughts, becomes revealed in its sublime and spiritual grandeur. Stop the stream of thoughts, if you can, and gaze steadily at the *Thinker*. Let the intellect take its repose, and watch attentively the vacuum in consciousness which would appear to be left.

The Overself consciousness is equivalent to the deep dreamless sleep state, with all its refreshment and peace, but instead of darkness and oblivion there is complete awareness. If we can only succeed in lifting the veil of unconsciousness which hangs over deep sleep we may discover the meaning of heaven on earth. And just as all thinking ceases in that state, so for the student entering this condition, all thoughts necessarily come to an end. It is hard for the European mind to conceive of such a state for man where consciousness exists without thought, but by practice and experience we may verify this.

The electron theory of modern science provides us with an apt analogy for the Overself. It represents the atom as a miniature universe resembling our solar system. At the centre of this atomic system we have a charge of positive electricity round which a cloud of negative electrical charges (the electrons) revolve. The positive and negative charges equilibrate each other, so that the atom does not ordinarily break up. Thus there is a positive charge at rest at the centre, and there are negative charges in motion round about that centre. The point of Absolute Rest round which the electrons revolve may be likened to the true self, and the electrons to its appurtenances, intellect, emotion, body. The Overself of man is *changeless*.

To find the soul is simply to recur to our original state. Purely divine beings we were in some far-off past, but untrammelled by the coverings of thought and body. Divine beings we are yet, but these later coverings have caused us to forget who we are. Hence to pierce through them is to see our proper self.

We must experience ourselves as we really are—not as prisoners in the body, as captives in the cage of thoughts or fettered by fleeting passions. Our consciousness is pinned down by these various forms. The whole art of meditation and concentration consists of unlocking our chains and rising up as free spirits.

In an old Indian writing I read the lines:

"Because I had forsaken unity with thee,
  Because I, fool, had made my body me,
  Because I did not know thee who didst dwell in me,
  Therefore I wandered through raging hells. . . .
  Because I threw away my very self, I therefore was in chains."

§

The discovery of a new cinema "star" is hailed through the press of the entire world as a great event, but the discovery of a man's spiritual self takes place in utter silence, without the world's praise or its printed record.

This path leads on to abiding quietude. Deeper and deeper must we penetrate, with focussed mind, until we enter the realm where this blessed quietude reigns. A great peace will slowly invade your inner being, a strange holy quietness will increasingly make itself felt.

You will know that you are coming into the aura of the true self by the experience of a happy feeling. This is but the initial stage. The last is to have ecstatic union.

Little by little, all the impressions of your immediate surroundings will be cut away, the world and its affairs will begin to recede, for when our minds are withdrawn from the hurried turmoil of our times and find their native state in such quiet moments, they become starred with sublime peace.

As we pass into the inmost centre of our mind, we arrive at a state where thought itself stops still, and where there seems at first to be nothing—except the blissful consciousness of Being, the sublime repose in Infinite Existence. This is the self that we really are, the Overself

> "Turning away from the world,
> I have forgotten both caste and lineage,
> My weaving is now in the infinite silence.
> Kabir, having searched and searched himself,
> Hath found God within him"

—these lines were written many hundreds of years ago by Kabir, the poet-weaver of Benares.

When, in our meditations, we seek to trace out the true "I" and not merely sink in slothful acceptance of its manifold masks, we eventually arrive at an inner state which is really the most interesting in life.

It is not unconsciousness. It is not sleep. It is not dream. Within its strange clasp we become conscious of an intense awareness of infinitude. Entry into this condition temporarily transfigures a man's entire nature. We discard the petty and personal, and discover our illimitable and divine nature. When we retire into the citadel of the soul the moving panorama of sense-impressions begins to fade out of sight. As we enter intimately into ourselves, the picture of the world which held us enchanted and robbed us of true self-consciousness, begins to disappear. When we put the mind in repose and recollect who we are our effort needs no further reward. We have secured balm for the day and all life looks good. When the human mind stops its incessant action; when it empties itself of every image and idea, then does it become a clear mirror in which the ineffable Divinity reflects itself.

Our grave and learned sceptics will tell us that these spiritual ecstasies are mere derangements of the nervous system; their cold brothers, the medicos, may likewise affix some such label as excessive blood-pressure, or what not. Others will mistake these records for the introspective musings of a solitary dreamer. But, rather than reject these glimpses of the glorious possibilities of man with the contemptuous prejudice of misunderstanding, it were better for them to admit that they are too strange for their wits to follow, and thus quietly dismiss them for the while.

Men may sit in solemn conclave to investigate these assertions, as some will. They would be wiser, however, if they investigated their own selves. For the experience of the eternal being within is its own best proof.

It is in this strange manner that the man who follows this path of self-analytical meditation first awakens to the guidance of his intuition. When he begins to feel the in-leading that will surely arise in the depths of his being; when he begins to yield himself utterly to it and lets it draw his consciousness still further into himself; when he willingly surrenders his personal thoughts, memories and feelings and lets them drown in the impersonal current of life which has mysteriously arisen of its own accord; when he submits to this profound guidance, he will be led right across the threshold of self-knowledge into the inner chamber where his real self awaits him. Once he gets even a momentary experience of this kind, he will understand something of what I mean when I speak of the spiritual being of man. He will realize that he has passed into a wonderful condition without the use of the five senses, without dreaming even; into something that is *real*, and transforming, and which he has never before experienced.

In the cathedral-like silence of the soul, he will feel that merely to think is to make a sacrilegious noise. In this lofty mood, when he discovers the presence of his diviner self, he realizes he can best pay for the privilege by gathering all thoughts into a heap upon the sacred altar and sacrificing them. In this strange moment the intellect temporarily cremates itself, and out of its ashes rises the phœnix of the true self, the imperishable Overself of man.

## CHAPTER VIII

THE AWAKENING TO THE OVERSELF

WHOEVER has patiently practised the exercises in meditation prescribed in this book and has thereby won through to the inner contact with his diviner self, will no longer need to repeat these exercises in the identical manner which he has heretofore followed. The minute analysis of self which has been the burden of his oft-repeated efforts becomes unnecessary and is eventually replaced by a more or less swift indrawing of the mind, which occurs soon after the student has put himself in silence and composed his thoughts. That is to say, once having arrived at the strong inner conviction that body, emotion and intellect are not himself, he need no longer repeat the technique of self-analysis in his meditations. He need only practise the breathing exercise which has been given and then place his mind in the half-question, half-prayer condition which is described in the preceding chapter. After the necessary pause, the waiting period of humble expectancy, the response of the Overself will usually be forthcoming and he will temporarily enter the state of partial or complete inner illumination. For a brief while he will stand still in the centre of his being, letting go completely of the frets and frictions of personal life, and returning to conscious integrality.

The stream of mental quiet has at last carried him beyond the intellect.

I shall not take the traveller on the Secret Path far across this threshold. Whatever happens to him henceforth will be an individual matter, and if he has had the courage and patience to come thus far, he will draw to himself the right guidance he may further need. Few ever cross far into this mystic realm but most adventurers linger on the threshold, content with its seraphic brightness, its spiritual warmth and its unutterable peace.

But it is now necessary to utter a warning. If, in the foregoing outline of the Secret Path, I have given the impression that Self-knowledge is a subject which one masters merely by practising certain exercises, obeying certain rules and studying certain ideas, precisely as one masters a mundane subject like physical culture, the student would not have formed a true concept of what is required. So strangely subtle and peculiarly delicate are the moods which he has to invoke, that something more than conforming to a prescribed system is required. And that final but important ingredient he himself is powerless to supply.

The awakening to spiritual consciousness is something which cannot be developed by a mechanical and measured system alone. "Art happens!" declared Ruskin, and so does spirituality. The aspirant carries on certain practices, whether meditation or relaxation, whether self-observation or self-remembering; carries on his effort of Interrogative Reflection, and one day the true consciousness seems to come to him, quietly, gently but surely. That day cannot be predetermined. It may come early in his efforts; it may come only after long years of disappointing struggle. . . . For it depends upon a manifestation of Grace from the Overself, of a force deeper than his personal will, which now begins to take a hand in this celestial game. Once the Grace gets to work upon a man, there is no escape. Quietly, gradually, but perceptibly, it draws him *inwards*.

The word Grace is not one I am over-keen to use. It has so many unpleasant and inaccurate theological connotations that, could I but find a better, I would throw it aside. But I cannot. So I shall endeavour to assign it a meaning based on ascertainable spiritual experience and not on blind belief.

*Grace* is the essential pre-requisite for enlightenment. Yet you cannot supply it; *only your Overself or a true Adept can do that*. Grace may fall with astonishing and unexpected celerity on a man who has lived what the world would call a sinful life, and change his heart, mind and consciousness very rapidly. Grace may withhold itself from a man who has spent twenty years studying tome after tome upon religion and philosophy. Its operation is often obscure, sometimes sudden and mysterious, and not infrequently a secret to other men. Yet for all this it is not an arbitrary force; it possesses its own laws and ways of working, but only a true Adept is in a position to ascertain them all.

To obtain this Grace we must ask for it. This is not to say that the asking is done by verbal action alone. That may suffice for some; for others, the request may be uttered mentally only. But for most of us we must ask with our whole life. Our course of action, our sacrifices of the primrose path, our surrender of time even, should show and express this great desire. And we may even be forced down on our knees, at unexpected hours of the night or day, to pray that the Light be granted us. If this happens, do not resist or resent it. Yield, and if you feel an urge to weep when praying for the Overself's Grace, then let the tears flow as copiously as they come forth. Do not hold them back. There is great spiritual merit in weeping for the visitation of a higher power. Each tear will dissolve something that stands between you and the divine union. Never be ashamed of such tears, for they fall in a good cause.

I have heard of few who win Grace without toil and sacrifice. Those few who receive it seemingly as a sudden gift, dropped from the skies, provide no exception to the rule of asking. Only—their aspiration was uttered and heard in former existences, in earlier "body-births." Destiny has something to do with the matter and provides her detailed explanations of apparently erratic behaviour only to those keen souls who have won her secret.

When Grace raises from our own Overself the latter sets up a certain urge in the heart and begins to lead our thoughts into certain channels. We become dissatisfied with our life as it is; we begin to aspire to something better; we commence a quest for a higher Truth than the belief which has hitherto held us. We imagine—and naturally—that the change is due to a developing mind or, sometimes, to changing circumstance. But not so. Veiled behind the mystery that is Life moves the unseen Overself, the august Being who has thus strangely interrupted our mortal sleep. The very quest for Truth was simply a quest for the Overself. Mayhap we find a worthier philosophy of life and thus come a little closer to true self-realization. But the uplifting thoughts and moods of that changing period—whether a week or years—are merely a manifestation of Grace, or if I may put it paradoxically, the results of an inner movement made by the Motionless.

Hard to grasp this truth, that the aspirational call must come to us; we do not stir it into sound of our own accord. We must cast ourselves prostrate at the feet of the Real Self and pray for its grace. When the fire of divine aspiration awakens in our heart, we may know that some modicum of Grace has been granted to us.

We who are servitors of that high king must wait upon his mood. Grace is a gift, a favour to be received at the hands of the god within. It cannot descend at any arbitrary moment, however. It usually comes when the necessary bodily, environmental and experiential conditions are ripe. The spirit takes its own time, not ours. For——

> "We cannot kindle when we will
> The fire which in the heart resides;
> The Spirit bloweth and is still
> In mystery the soul abides."
> MATTHEW ARNOLD.

The ripening of the soul for this profound experience of union with the Overself takes place gradually, as does the ripening of fruit. But once the growth is complete, then union overwhelms the soul with sudden downpouring and man is really born anew.

§

There are certain root experiences which a man never forgets. The first day he loves a woman is one of them. The first day he lands on a foreign shore is another. And the first time he breaks the chrysalis of being to emerge as a conscious spiritual unit, is a third—and it is the greatest of all.

The Overself makes no demand of man other than that he open his inner eyes and perceive its existence. Yet the day of that vision is the most starred day of his whole life, for on that day he stands on the edge of eternity.

For this he was really born, and not merely to mend shoes or traffic in figures. If he misses this divine experience, even then Nature will not let him escape. She is in no hurry, however. Somewhere in her spacious realm she will yet catch him and compel him to fulfil her secret purpose. Whoever engages in such inward exploration is no dreamer: he merely antedates to-day what the multitude of men will have perforce to do to-morrow.

Memorable is the grandeur of that august moment when he first beholds the divinity which environs him, but which, paradoxically, is also at the kernel of his being. In the "ecstasy of quietude," as Rupert Brooke called it, he learns to know what he truly is. As James Rhoades expresses it in beautiful verse:

"I am thy Dawn, from darkness to release:
I am the Deep, wherein thy sorrows cease:
Be still! be still! and know that I am God:
Acquaint thyself with Me, and be at peace!

Erase that record of the palimpsest
Within thee, by the scribe of time impressed:
And on the smoothed surface write anew:
'I am All-Wisdom, Righteousness, and Rest.'

I am alone: thou only art in Me:
I am the stream of Life that flows through thee:
I comprehend all substance, fill all space:
I am pure Being, by whom all things be.

Yes, I am Spirit: in thy depths I dwell:
Art conscious of My presence, all is well:
Cleave but to that—thyself art thine own heaven,"
                                        *Out of the Silence*

Once we push the gate of the mind slightly ajar and let the light stream in, the meaning of life becomes silently revealed to us. The gate may be open for one minute or for one hour, but in that period we discover the secret and neither weary time nor bitter woe can tear that priceless knowledge away from us. Words fall dead when I try to express that meaning, but whoever has felt his whole inner being melt away and dissolve into the mysterious Infinite during such meditation, as a result of constant aspiration or by the Grace of some Adept, will understand this thought I am feebly trying to convey. In the still presence of that mighty power the soul walks on tip-toe.

It is the most wonderful moment in a man's or woman's life, this illumination of the heart and mind.

Find yourself—your Overself, and you will begin to find the meaning of life and begin to unveil the mystery of the universe. Back of each one of us there is this Overself—

calm as an unruffled sky, wise with the gathered experience of Nature's many million years of existence, strong with a power to bring you the best which life has to offer. Let me recall the words of one who was perfectly aware of it—a humble carpenter turned Teacher and who wandered along the shores of Galilee with a few disciples over nineteen hundred years ago. He told them: "Ask and it shall be given to you; seek and ye shall find; knock, and it shall be opened unto you."

These words are as true to-day as they were then. The man-god who spoke them is seemingly gone from our midst, but the divine truths to which He gave voice will always remain with mankind.

Those of us who have taken this peep through the door of our own being, are dumbfounded. We draw back, surprised, at the inscrutable possibilities of the Overself. Man as a spiritual being possesses a capacity for wisdom which is infinite, a resource of happiness which is startling. He contains a divine infinitude within himself, yet he is content to go on and potter about a petty stretch of life as though he were a mere human insect.

When a man reaches the apex of truth he is able to enjoy his own being, to gain from within that happiness which he has hitherto sought amid external things. Truth, Beauty, Peace, Power and Wisdom are all attributes of the Overself —that self which awaits our finding. The divine self imparts whatever of idealism, insight, and nobility is present in us. We have yet to learn the true meaning of the verb "to be."

In the deeps of our miraculous being we may discover that we are parts of a great life whose condition is peace eternal, whose purpose is utterly benevolent and whose existence can never perish.

Yes, this is the true "home-state" of every man.

This timeless condition in which we discover ourselves has been beautifully described by the Hindu Sages as "The Eternal Now."

"Who knows his own nature knows heaven," declared Mencius, the Chinese disciple of Confucius.

The spiritual self of man remains unaltered and undisturbed in all its grandeur, while his personal self passes through the greatest vicissitudes of fortune. It is the indestructible element in him, the silent and eternal witness to whom he must one day come and render homage. It is a light which no power can extinguish. It is man's immortal spirit, benign and tolerant, beautiful and unchanging.

We are as close to the god within as we ever shall be. All we need to do is to know this by experiment and experience. The Soul broods in secret over its great treasure; let us come to rest in the centre of our being and discover the diamonds and rubies that are hid.

The Overself is the true being, the divine inhabitant of this body, the Silent Witness within the breast of man. Man lives every moment in the presence of this divine self, but the membrane of ignorance hangs over him and covers sight and sense. This doctrine is one of the most difficult to justify. How explain to mortal, troubled man that the spiritual self can exist serenely apart, self-sufficing, untouched and untrammelled by any external condition? I fear this statement must look foolish to one who quakes at sight of misfortune or brightens at tidings of external good. How dare I tell him that he is self-hypnotized into despair or elation, and yet that he remains paradoxically free of both? The "man of the world" will ridicule this assertion, while the theologian may reject it.

There is but one final answer to this puzzling riddle, one supreme authority to whom it can be referred for solution. And that is, the authority of one's personal experience, one's own first-hand realization that these things are true.

Knowledge of the self is the absolute and all-essential basis for knowledge of the Truth. Our first and foremost thought is of self in the sense of "I." Trace this thought down to its source, and when you have found THAT in which it arises, you will have found the Overself, Truth, Wisdom—God!

§

Some will object that the inner shrine is shrouded in darkness and that the way thereto is impassable. No, we must not be intimidated by such fears. The sanctuary is not impenetrable and if few appear to have found it in these days, it is because few have begun to search for it.

Truth is written into the organism of man no less surely than into the inspired books. In the spacious society of the universe, man possesses a better status than he is yet aware of. Mostly in moments of secret mental quiet are hints brought to him concerning the grandeur which is native to the soul.

This wisdom is the oldest wisdom in the world. Far back as our foremost minds can peer, before the first pen was ever put to paper, ages beyond Buddha and Zoroaster, this single and simple Truth that man can consciously unite with the divine while in the body was taught to those who aspired.

The universality of the experience which I have described is authentic testimony to its reality. The literatures of all lands, the philosophies and religions of all times, bear witness to its truth. It appears in the pages of Grecian Plato and American Emerson; it is to be found in the philosophies of Roman Porphyrus and German Fichte, it haloes the sayings of Syrian Jesus and lights the words of Indian Buddha.

To the real Seer all creeds come alike; those who profess the faith of Buddha are not less welcome than those who profess the faith of Christ.

"The entertaining of a single thought of a certain elevation makes all men of one religion. It is always some base alloy that creates the distinction of sects. Thought meets thought over the widest gulf of time with unerring freemasonry. I know, for instance, that Sadi entertained once identically the same thought that I do, and hereafter I can find no essential difference between Sadi and myself. He is not Persian, he is not ancient, he is not strange to me. By the identity of his thoughts with mine he still survives," said Henry David Thoreau, with truth.

Different people in different lands have given this secret experience different names. Some Christians have called it "Union with God," while Hindu saints name it "Union with the spirit-self." Some philosophers describe it as "merging into the infinite," and others as "finding truth." The label is not important: the wise will never quarrel over it, for words hint at but cannot describe the fullness of this experience.

Hindu and Hebrew mystic, Platonic and Pythagorean philosopher, Chinese and Christian moralist—all speak the same language and talk in the same tones if we but hear them aright. No matter how different are the creeds nor how numerous the theologies may be, God was, is and can be, but the Primal One.

Truth is the spiritual white light which falls upon the prism of mankind, and breaks into the many colours whereby individuals interpret it. Thus, the experience of discovering it is the same the world over: what differs is the interpretation thereof.

Some will object that the world has received a bewildering array of reports from its mystics, from those who claim to have "gone inwards" yet return with varying accounts of what they have experienced, witnessed, felt and understood.

The admixture of religious dogmas and the misinterpretation of personal experiences have produced the bewildering mass of doctrines which, in the lump, is called "mystical." The inability to adopt a strictly scientific attitude towards the whole matter is responsible for the obfuscation of meditation's first object. Various "paths" have been devised to secure this object but a multitude of narrow minds have mistaken the path for the goal. Meditation, Yoga, mysticism, etc., have only one fundamental purpose, whatever prejudiced exponents or mistaken adherents may say. That purpose is to short-circuit the currents of thinking so that one may perceive the reality which thought obscures. In other words, advanced religious practices, methods of meditation, ecstatic saint worship, etc., are all means to help man slow down the stream of thoughts until he eventually stops its flow completely. Sectarian mentalities will, of course, vehemently object to this, but their denial is simply a denial of the true facts. Mature and penetrating souls alone can perceive this truth. They alone, by clarifying their understanding of this subject, can escape from the spiritual fog wherein most students and devotees habitually move. They alone know that the particular religious path anyone follows has less to do with his attainment than the mechanical method of mind control he unconsciously practises. They alone know that the absence of any creed whatsoever from his beliefs makes a man no less successful than his more pious brother.

What the advanced Indian Yogi experiences as Nirvana, is substantially the same condition as what the advanced Christian mystic experiences as God. If either, in recording or describing this sublime state, tacks on to it theological or local doctrines peculiar to his race or land, we must ascribe these accretions to their true source—the personal prejudices or mental bias of the seer—and not to the illumination itself.

Illumination, in its varying degrees, is the same for all men alike. Every mystic rediscovers the same hidden treasure, but his description of it may be lamentably different because his intellectual and emotional interpretation of it is different. *There are degrees of illumination itself,* and in the most advanced degree all seers obtain the same experience and agree perfectly in its understanding. But such are the rare few, the gifted immortals among men.

Temporary glimpses and experiences of a mystical nature have occurred in every century and in every land; but intelligent interpretation of these experiences is not so plentiful. The kindergarten alphabet of every creed has been dragged in to explain them, and that which descends out of the Universal and Infinite is chained to some local symbol.

Our time demands a sensible and spiritual explanation of these things, not an unscientific and religio-materialistic one. Visionaries have recorded perfectly genuine experiences, both psychic and spiritual, yet they differ widely in their results; why? Because the beliefs with which they started out, the past experiences which have influenced their personalities, all these have influenced the interpretation of their results. The interpretation may be unsound, therefore, when the inner experience is quite valid.

We make the mistake of attempting to erect a circumscribing fence around this divine discovery; through all ages genuine seekers, but with narrow minds or little experience have tried to force this wide ocean of Truth-knowledge into a small compound of doctrine or creed. It cannot be done, and when their experience deepens they themselves come to realize that this is so, but the frowns of orthodox churches or the difficulty of explaining such subtle truth to the multitude often compels their silence.

Creeds come and go, cults arise and slowly disappear, sects take the world's stage for a time but must ultimately make their exit, yet the ancient wisdom, stripped of its trappings of external expression, remains forever identical and unchanged. It is independent of race—witness Thoreau among the Americans and Sankara among the Hindus. It is apart from the centuries—Rabindranath Tagore to-day and Meister Eckhart over six hundred years ago. It is unaffected by climate—the fur-wrapped Tibetan hermit Milarepa dwelling on an icy plateau ultimately arrives at the same truth as Plotinus living in warmer clim'd Egypt. The same inward experience informed the beautiful Persian poems of Jelaluddin Rumi as inspired the haunting Christian verses of Francis Thompson. The inspirations of early Rome parallel the inspirations of early China. Similarities in all these are startling; thoughts are identical, but the vestures of those thoughts are necessarily subject to personal tastes and racial customs.

The simple and beautiful sayings of Jesus carry the burden of Truth's essential message. Study them well and you shall find they correspond completely with the sayings or writings of other men who are at one with the Overself. All the masters of deep spiritual realization speak alike: only the stumbling followers and professional theologians disagree and differ.

Do you imagine that God showed Himself to men only in those far-off days when Christ stirred up an obscure corner of the Roman Empire or when Buddha walked with the begging-bowl? If God cannot show Himself again to-day, then His power has become strangely circumscribed and the Absolute has suddenly shrunk back to the Finite. Is it not better to believe that He is ready to reveal Himself to all who care to fulfil the conditions precedent to revelation? The Eternal has spoken to man in the past and can speak to him again.

Who can explain the spell which men like Christ and Buddha flung over their auditors by means of a few words? Oratorical genius cannot explain it; intellectual genius cannot explain it. Something more than these things is required to make plain why their silent glances moved stony hearts which no eloquent perorations were ever likely to move, some mysterious possession of a power at once awe-inspiring and divine.

For centuries erudite scholars have trained their searchlights upon the story of Jesus. They have examined minutely every shred of information about Him, every source and every document that might make their vision of the mysterious Galilean a little clearer. And now, nearly two thousand years after the death of "the Inspired Jew," He remains still an enigmatic and unfamiliar figure. His biography is still largely imaginative, His personality has been pictured in a thousand contradictory ways, His teachings have been used to buttress opposing institutions. Yes, though the world still writes the name of this wonderful man with a certain veneration, still holds His high above every other name in the West, He remains a mystery.

The unaided intellect of man can never solve this mystery. Out of the divine Infinite He came to the tribes of men, gave his sacred words—and was gone. Such was the outer picture.

For Christ descended on earth from a superior planet, which was His real home, and which is far ahead of ours in spiritual consciousness, to bless and serve men by His presence. This descent was His real cross, His real crucifixion. And those who sincerely seek Him may still find Him—in their hearts.

But divinity was not buried in the tomb with Jesus. Have no holy voices spoken since then? Can we not search history for the past two thousand years and find the names of a few men whose presence and look testified to lofty spiritual attainment? Is not the deeper life always extending its sublime invitation to us?

§

Why should we hide these simple truths under a complicated jargon? Why should we dress this beautiful figure of Truth in coarse sackcloth. Men like Buddha and Jesus did not disdain to expound their thought in clear-cut phrase and to explain their meaning in simple words. The profounder thoughts can be simply expressed; it is not at all necessary to put them into prose of Cimmerian mystery. Yet there are those who delight in using a vocabulary and phraseology which build barriers between Truth and its mental understanding.

The stake and the gallows and the cross once waited for the spiritual pioneers who dared to utter heterodox thoughts; hence a jargon of obscure and guarded terminology grew up among some who walked this lone path. But there is no justification in this twentieth century for the weird jargon of medieval days still current in certain circles. The highest truths can now be revealed without fear of the hanging rope or the torture rack; why frighten simple truth-seekers by piling up complicated mysteries?

In former times this interior path and its results were

described in published books under poetical, symbolical and allegorical phrases. Such a style was of use to the intuitional who were able to read therein something which the unenlightened man could never perceive.

In the present era the time has come to speak more openly and more plainly of these matters. We live in an intellectual and scientific age when a set of teachings must be presented in a manner which will appeal to the ordered intelligence of men. Any other kind of presentation will cause such teachings to be treated as poetry, as a decoration for spare moments.

The prevalence of science and the popularization of knowledge have fostered man's intellect. Therefore a modern expression of truth must, at the least, make as strong an appeal to his mind as to his heart. The needs of the brain cannot be despised by any spiritual message nowadays, though they should never be permitted to play the despot.

We who have had first-hand experience of the amazing potentialities of meditation must be ready to meet the doubter on his own ground, and to free him who is a prisoner of the primitive conceptions that man is nothing more than his material body and that the world was formed from nothing more than the primeval mud. It is not enough to tell him that our stars burned a little brighter at our births; we must show him how he can kindle a greater light for himself too. If still he insists on shutting his eyes to the possibilities of man's life here and now, he will have no excuse for the spiritual darkness which environs him.

Yet there is little that is radically new here, in the historical sense; only the synthesis and proper proportioning of these thoughts will appear fairly fresh with this book; but everything that has not been tried out is new, and these things have not been tried by the world at large.

The trained modern intelligence demands and must receive a better presentation of truth than the mere aspirations of religio-moral sentimentality.

We must remember too that the teachers who came in the past, came to peoples whose mentalities were unlike our own, and came at times when the economic problems of industrial civilisation had not become so heavy as to press down upon all others. They came to Eastern peoples, who are naturally more sensitive than our own, whose minds are less sceptical and less restless, and whose hearts are habitually turned towards religious devotion. It must therefore be clear that the Seers of to-day, and of the West especially, should forget the presentations of the past in order to remember the needs of the present. Hence they will seek to give out expressions of truth suited to the times. Such expressions are already taking shape in various movements and cults, however partial they may be. So, too, in this teaching of spiritual self-inquiry it is needful to show what worth and value it possesses for those who are held captive by the perpetual agitation of modern life, and what "practical" application may be made of its fundamental principle that the real self of man is divine.

## CHAPTER IX

### THE WAY OF DIVINE BEAUTY

THERE are some temperaments which will find it almost impossible to take up this path of introspective self-analysis. Unfortunately, but not unnaturally, their minds are not built in a way that will permit them to hold their thoughts to such a topic. What, then, are they to do?

The way out of this difficulty for the student unattached to any personal teacher is to begin by yielding himself deliberately to the rhythm of inspired works of art, or by cultivating exalted moods induced in the presence of Nature's beauty, and by widening the feelings of veneration whenever they suffuse the soul through such external agencies.

A picture by a master hand, a poem by one who is sensitive to the spiritual side of life, the playing of a violin by a genius like Kreisler, a walk through gaunt leafless woods in autumn, a contemplation of the glint of June sunshine upon the honeysuckle, or the sight of an old church in the waning light of the westering sun—these things may move him to fine feelings of a kind which the ordinary activities of life do not usually call forth. There is a spiritual power in these moments which we remember long after they are gone. Rightly used they can become as Jacob's ladders leading from earth to heaven.

I have written elsewhere that to-day the inspired artist is taking up the burdens of the priest, through becoming the instrument of that aspect of the Higher Power which reveals itself to man as beauty.

The artist, the writer and the musician incarnates himself into his work, and if he is blessed at times with lofty inspirations, if he has striven to sound a spiritual note in the art of his time, if he has sat at the feet of divine beauty or true wisdom, then in the degree to which you yield yourself up to his influence shall you share those inspirations with him.

In every person's life there exist certain moments when the effect of art or nature is to produce an indefinable sense of great calm or a flowing tide of bliss which overwhelms him. What lies behind such ecstatic moments?

These are the moments in a man's life when he stands at the gate of the spirit, though he know it not. In the presence of some grand scene of Nature, he is unconsciously reminded of his true spiritual home; so grand, so beautiful is it. He loves the bright clouds in the sky and the golden sunsets, peaceful woodlands and calm lakes, because they remind him of his spiritual origin. Beauty speaks to him with these voices and says: "This grandeur is what you should attain inwardly." They are voices calling to him from his spiritual home.

Sometimes, as in listening to inspiringly fine music, to the noble melodies of Bach or the pure strains of Mozart, for instance, or gazing on some mountain scene, he receives hints of a higher life for man. Music, being the most direct of all the fine arts, provides the truest medium of spiritual expression. But, alas! he knows not the august nature of his visitants and they tremble away. If he had the leisure and desire to attend to the fine thoughts which troop after a moment of awe and wonder, even the average man might gradually become illumined.

For all fine art is but a symbol leading to a shrine of

golden fire; all inscribed inspirations are but the filmy veils which cover the naked body of Truth.

Those who try to gather into their minds the world's harvest of printed beauty and wisdom are moved to do so by an instinct that comes from afar. For when the eyes gaze upon a page written with literary art and shimmering with golden spiritual thoughts, a mysterious sense will be felt confirming that which is read.

When you approach the house of a really inspired scribe or musical composer and enter his room, you see no mere study but a veritable alchemist's workshop. Is he not the lonely magician who sits amid Olympian ways and watches the panorama of life as one apart? What is his pen but a wand of thaumaturgic power that evokes a hidden world of unexpected splendour before our profane eyes? Are not the writings that cover his table mysterious papyrii that embalm the sacred words of communion with a higher realm.

When he takes up the pen and wields it as a magic wand, casting it about our atmosphere and changing the heavy night that covers us into the growing dawn, he becomes, if only for a little while, as potent a wizard as those of old. The magicians of those times sought by a wave of the wand to bring men to see such things as they desired them to see. They touched a seed and it became a tree, or wrapped the Cloak of Invisibility about themselves. But now we have put aside such clumsy effects and seek to place subtle spells upon the mind of man with nothing more mysterious than a humble pen.

I have read books that filled my mind with golden images of such strange power that I lost the sense of being and became blent with brooding infinity. And who has not read other books wherein the intense vision of the writer so worked upon his thoughts that it evoked an ancient vanished civilization before his astonished gaze?

The student who finds himself most stirred by great literature should take a book, or some passages from a book, which makes a deep appeal to him, which seems to bring with it a breath of inspiration, which has an unfailingly exalting effect upon him, and which comes almost with the force of a message from higher regions. If he cares for great poetry and can feel its power he may find this inspiration in some haunting poem by Francis Thompson, in a sonnet by Shelley or a lyric by Keats, and in some of those shining verses by my gifted Irish friend, "A. E." (George W. Russell).[1]

If he prefers prose there are some delightful essayists to serve him, writers who raise the divine spark of creative art and set fire to the tinder of man's imagination. Emerson's essay on self-reliance, for example, holds at the least a hundred quotable sentences. He is one of the most original and most perceptive thinkers among the moderns. His pithy thoughts fall like nuggets of gold from his pen. Spend an hour with him and you are received into the company of the great. Enter into his high mood and you enter into an atmosphere reminiscent of the Upanishads, the Tripitakas, the New Testament and the Platonic books; you breathe *truth* from the very beginning. He quibbles no argument and faces every thought; he wants the raw truth about a matter, and nothing less. His Palladian pages are inspiring to the last syllable.

If the student can give his sympathy to ancient scriptures he will find in the sublime sayings of Christ, in the illuminating dialogues of Buddha and in the translations of the Hindu "Bhagavad Gita" or "Lord's Song" sources of profound help.

Let him select a paragraph or fragment from these or any ancient or modern book which makes most appeal to him and ruminate mentally over it, reverently trying to suck out its meaning, as it were, trying to enter into the spiritual rhythm or mental wave-length which brought it to birth. Let him do this with the utmost slowness, with the utmost absorption that he can muster, holding the heart as well as the mind to the chosen passage, while the words vibrate in his soul.

Do not read the words alone; read the thoughts behind them also.

Concentrate as you read. Read slowly by letting each word sink into your consciousness. And as it sinks let its meaning pass into your mind also. Repeat each word mentally in such a way that you actually become the author, the creator, as it were. You, yourself, construct the sentences and form the paragraphs—this is creative and con-

---

[1] *The Oxford Book of English Mystical Verse* (published by Oxford University Press) contains several poems of this kind.

structive reading. It brings grist to the mill of your mind and food for the brain. Such reading literally engraves itself into your thoughts. You have set your own mind to work, to think along the lines and tracks indicated by the author.

The basic thing is to concentrate upon some abstract idea, some phrase or verse, that the student is able to experience within his mind in a powerful way, that echoes deeply within the chambers of his soul. He must choose such passages as have this effect upon him, even though other persons might find only words in them. He must feel the presence of an element of inspiration quite apart from the literary value of the piece or poem.

There are certain paragraphs which stand up like peaks in such books. They are the passages wherein the author has written wiser than he knew, written I should say, under the inspiration of his spiritual self.

These enchanted and enchanting hours when you are caught in a mood of exalted calm or emotional wonderment by a piece of writing which overwhelms you, which is spirit made words, must be watched and caught at their profoundest moment. You must not dissipate these fine feelings, but rather treasure them as being of the utmost value. You must not hurry away quickly to the next impression. You should hold your attention in this mood. This is the high and serene moment when the book can be laid aside, for it has done its work. Pause, and prepare to pass through the beautiful gate of symbol into the starry world beyond. But if the gate is closed to you and its fastenings too cunning for your eyes, despair not; rest awhile and pray. Perchance the hidden guardian of the threshold will come forth with his simply-fashioned key and unlock the shadowed entrance for you.

Pause, at this mysterious moment, and begin to practise the exercise in placid breathing, and then follow the instructions given upon the awakening to intuition.

The student can also penetrate into this element by other paths. He must choose the medium whose power he feels most. It is not essential, therefore, to take a book, since our aim is but to evoke a high mood, to free the mind for a while of all personal affairs, and to abstract it from the usual run of worldly activities. He might get equal results by listening to music composed by true genius. One personality will arrive at this inner mood through a book, another through music, and so on. The essential thing is to profit by the exalted mood in the manner indicated in the foregoing paragraph.

## CHAPTER X

### THE GOSPEL OF INSPIRED ACTION

"CAN we reduce such uncommon thoughts as these to the common needs of the hour?" you will ask. "We cannot desert the world, cannot leave our Londons and go forth to contemplation amid solitude; we have our debts to pay to Admetus and our feet are chained for life while paying them," you will complain. "The world is harsh and hard and has no use for such vain and hollow doctrines as yours. We cannot subsist upon a diet of clouds. Yours is an excellent philosophy for those who sit in ease at the chimney-corner, perhaps, but how can it help us who toil and moil amid a matter-of-fact society?" you will conclude.

These questions contain some frequent misconceptions of what constitutes true spirituality and I shall begin to answer them by posing another question in return.

"Have you ever been caught up in one of those tropical whirlwinds which move with awe-inspiring force?"

Strangely enough, you find that, in the very centre of the whirlwind, there is a place perfectly calm and untouched. So, too, the man who knows himself attains mental equilibrium and remains unmoved amid the feverish activity of the world. His inmost being is in peaceful undisturbed repose, whatever whirlwind of life swirls around him, whatever work he is doing and whatever thoughts engage his intellect.

Spiritual truth is apt to be considered the prerogative of speculative men, lost in pious or philosophical dreams. That it should be brought within the purview of active men of affairs is a consideration which seems dubious but history has not infrequently turned it to fact.

Is it possible to fuse the wisdom of this world with the wisdom of things divine? Why not? Why, for instance, should not the spiritual seeker be conjoined with the man of business? I know one man who owns a chemical factory in an English provincial town who has attempted this. His entire organization, his laboratory equipment, his office equipment, his advertising methods and his manufactured products are easily among the best and most up-to-date in their line. He treats his many workers on the basis of the Golden Rule. There is nothing, within reason, that he will not do for them, with the result that there is nothing reasonable that they will not do for him. Every night before retiring to rest after the dust and effort of the day—for that is the only time he can spare—he goes off to a quiet corner of his house and devotes a tranquil half-hour to mental quiet, finding therefrom a sublime peace and supporting power which inspire his next day's activities, and which enable him to keep a secret liberty of the spirit amid all the mechanization of to-day. He has made this regular practice quite compatible with active life. It provides him with an inner poise amid the distractions and turmoil of present day existence. The higher wisdom and strength which he finds in the divine centre are later brought into effective action in his business.

The business man who objects that he has no time and no thoughts for spiritual interests because his material affairs absorb them all, is in a sorry plight. What then is the true business of man?

It is right to consider our material needs of the moment, but it is not right to consider them without reference to anything else.

Many are the Westerners who have buried themselves in their business and scarcely ever come out to notice that there is a spiritual sun above. A thousand thoughts throng their heads from dawn till dusk; the night falls and they are left to reap the harvest of what has been sown. Amid all this teeming field of thought and life—what remains? Even when danger threatens and the physician packs them off on a long holiday, such is their slavery that, though they cannot take the business with them, they are compelled to carry it in their minds; it is now the driver and they are but burdened steeds.

It is a sad but necessary day in a man's life when he

finds that, for all his striving, his hands hold little more than withered leaves. At such a moment he may begin to perceive that true spirituality is neither an abstract science nor an abstruse speculation; it is a way of life, a deeper outlook upon the world. It may be painful to arrive at such a day, but it is the prelude to a worth while happiness.

The practical affairs of human life no longer exist to serve them but to tyrannize over them. "Things are in the saddle and ride mankind," says Emerson somewhere, and it is true enough of such men. The consciousness that could be set free for a short while each day to acquire the jewel of inward spiritual peace is compelled by the machine they have constructed around themselves to grind itself out in the petty and the puerile.

Man, eager to improve his machines, forgets to improve himself.

To divorce life from the spiritual is to put it in danger. The active self must be fed by the spiritual resources of the deeper self. We must balance up by poising activity with our contemplation. The critical intellect must meet the visionary intuition as a friend, not as a foe; the commercial capacities must collaborate with the spiritual imaginations; while our deep selfishness needs to come to grips with our deeper altruism. In this way each of us can become the exponent of a deep viewpoint in our shallower life.

Our lives must find the golden mean. We must dwell awhile in mental quiet each day, without losing the capacity for practical work. We must put a proper balance upon the mystical and material elements of our nature, diverse and incompatible as they apparently are. Whoever will follow the Secret Path which has been outlined here will find this balance without strain. For it will come to him naturally of its own accord.

The monk who makes his meditation an obsession is free to do so; but we who have to live and work in the world must seek a wise balance. The light found during our practice of mental quiet will then shine through our actions when we go out to mingle freely with the crowd.

Inspired action can be made as much a practical exercise for attaining spirituality as renunciation of worldly life and retreat into monastic places. All the spiritual men do not wear monkish robes. Some wear tweed trousers!

Times change and men with them. The sequestered life

which satisfied the life-weary Eastern hermit of the past, will hardly satisfy the aspiring Western man of to-day. He cannot fail to feel somewhat of the spirit of material enterprise which surrounds him. If he is wide-awake he will know its value and consider how it may be conjoined to the higher aim which he has found. He need not lose sight of the practical affairs of life while he is engaged upon the mystical affairs of Truth.

A common idea of one who follows a spiritual path is that he is a pious and peaceful enough sort of man, but devoid of any sort of utility in the scheme of things, and defunct in the faculties of reason and common-sense. That he could link thought with thought in iron strictness, or go out and make a place for himself among the executives of a mammoth modern business, or command an entire battalion during war, is a notion which provokes satire, although I have known men of this kind who have done these things. He is looked upon as a somewhat feeble and foolish creature, even if a good-natured one.

"Because you are a devotee of God, does that mean you should be a fool? Do you think a shopkeeper opens a shop to practise religion? Why did you not examine the pan before you purchased it?" exclaimed Sri Ramakrishna, one of nineteenth-century India's most famous saints, to a young disciple who went out to buy an iron pot and, on returning, found it leaky.

The man who takes to the higher life is not necessarily emasculated of all human talent. Even if he becomes as humble and as loving as St. Francis of Assisi; he can still be as brainy as Bernard Shaw, as full of courage as William Tell, and as gifted as Galileo. It is false to believe that because he draws his wisdom by direct awareness from a deeper source, he need lose the ability to think logically, to manage both men and affairs, and to take his place in the active world. These qualities may still exist within him, but can no more enslave him.

To inspire one's daily life with strength drawn from faith in the divinity within, is surely to become a better worker, and not a worse. For then one has infinite power to draw upon, as well as greater wisdom to act rightly.

Sir J. A. Thompson in a recent Presidential address to the British Association, mentioned that the solution of some of his most intricate scientific problems came to him when he emptied his mind of the problems and let it remain quiet and still for a time.

Few know that the late Lord Leverhulme, who built up the largest industrial organization of its kind in the world, could relax anywhere at will and put himself into a serene state of reverie. In the midst of the most gigantic tasks he frequently availed himself of this power.

Those who believe that meditation rightly conducted in the way prescribed is only a form of sentimental idealism or abstract thinking, make a great mistake. Such meditation gradually liberates a soul-force in man of which he was not previously aware, and which eventually becomes the greatest inspirer of his activities. It is the most powerful precisely because it is the most inward element of his being.

This is a truth, and men like Oliver Cromwell, Abraham Lincoln and the Emperor Marcus Aurelius in the West, or like Prince Shivaji, the Emperor Akbar and King Asoka in the East, believed it, acted upon it and triumphed.

§

Man moves from morning till night across a background of activities and interests which are purely material in nature. In this, of course, he is acting quite naturally. The world confronts him ceaselessly and he must make what he can of it. But what he does not know is that by detaching himself for a very short space of time each day, by letting all his interests in these activities temporarily die out during that time he may obtain high protection and right guidance for all those activities.

The world gives itself up to incessant activity merely because it knows of nothing better. The inspired man works among its whirring wheels also but he knows whither the wheels are going. For he has found the Centre where all is stillness, where all is power, where all is wisdom, and for him the circumference of activity merely follows the Centre by natural law.

Our practical activity surrounds us with a close net; we need to free ourselves and yet not destroy the use of this useful net at the same time.

It is neither necessary nor sensible for the student to live with his head in the clouds. He is living on this mundane sphere and he best can express the principles he has learnt by applying them to his mundane existence. He needs to look up to the skies and gain the clear vision of spiritual insight, but after that he needs to look down on this earth again and apply that insight to the manner in which he handles his worldly affairs. He must endeavour to maintain an equilibrium between spiritual and material forces. He needs to achieve a balanced life; the life of the spirit sought and found daily and feeding the life of personal activity, and infusing its wisdom and power into his excursions into worldly affairs.

If he has regularly practised the meditations prescribed in the earlier pages, if he has constantly tried to gather his thoughts around the quest for the divine self, he will gradually become aware of the spiritual nature within himself which has hitherto been "covered over." I say "gradually" because wisdom does not arrive to a man on some precise day. It dawns.

This awareness is like the lighting of an electric lamp. A current of spirituality will be switched on with every such return to mental quiet or to self-observation. Let him attend to his duties and take his pleasures just as he did before. There need be no change in them other than what his gradual inner enlightenment will suggest. But then all such changes will be voluntary, not forced on him by an artificial system of external discipline.

Once he has established the habit of morning meditation, it becomes a perfectly natural thing to carry on all the day's activities within the spiritual current so started.

He will discover that his work will increasingly be carried out within this current of spirituality, which will last longer and longer into the day as he proceeds upon the Secret Path. Ultimately all his work, all his social relaxation will go on inside this current. His whole attitude will be changed by the presence of the current, but his work need not be neglected. And ultimately a time will come when he can drop his meditations because his whole life will be one long meditation—and yet he will be as active as ever!

Life will be enriched, and not lessened, if we draw upon this ancient wisdom. It supplements and complements; it need not destroy. We live chiefly for economic ends, but these can only be rightly achieved when we have permitted some spiritual impulses to filter down into them.

The spirit must enter into every department of a man's

life. If he leaves it out of his business activities, if he forgets it when he begins to think of sex, if he cannot express it when dealing with other people, he shuts himself out of its magical power to give him the truest success, the greatest happiness and the most harmonious existence.

Once we end this impossible division of interests and unify our scattered desires by a sublime sacrificial act of submission to the Higher Will, we may find peace. Once we bring ourselves to the final point of surrender to the promptings of the Overself, we begin to walk the path of our true destiny, our true life.

We shall lose nothing by obeying such promptings. There is room in life for the warmth of love as well as for the coldness of ascetic self-denial, for the hubbub of crowds as well as for the quiet of meditation. No modern way of higher living must be too spiritual to perform a few variations on such themes as worldly business and daily work, nor too refined to touch the piano keys of human love and human passion. In the result a time will arrive when the spiritual man will come to look upon everything, every object, event and person, as a manifestation of the Divine, when he will discover that he can have no higher commission than this—to express his Overself in whatever he does and with whoever he contacts.

Let us accept and use wisely all the facts which modern science has found out. Let us live in enjoyment of all the comforts and conveniences its progress can bestow. Let us renounce nothing but the unwise and destructive use we have often put it to, the unbalanced attention we have given it.

But let us also link this external social activity with a deeper life, the life of tranquil thought and inner peace, and thus learn to preserve an unruffled stillness of spirit even amid varied vicissitudes of existence.

Whoever has to live and work amid the busy and feverish life of to-day, for him too there is thus a way which leads straight to the calmness of the Supreme. Let him introduce into this distracting activity of a spiritualizing principle. Let him not renounce his work and flee from the haunts of men, but let him renounce his former attitude to work. That which was previously done for selfish benefit alone, is henceforth to be done also in the spirit of serving humanity. This is practical spirituality. Withal he will find half an hour each day wherein to collect high and holy ideas and place them upon the altar of his mind—a silent offering to the First Cause.

This is the only gospel which the practical West can use—this gospel of inspired action—if it is to attain a higher civilization.

If there is any message the whole world is waiting for, it is an East-West message, a gospel of Inspired Action!

Then we shall attack the world's problems of poverty, war, disease and ignorance with a new zest, and with better success, yet we shall not forget to render our daily homage to that peace-bestowing and soul-ennobling divinity who dwells in the hearts of men.

# CHAPTER XI

### SPIRITUAL HELP IN MATERIAL AFFAIRS

THE criticism will be offered by some who have read all the earlier chapters that these ideas may be very beautiful and profound, but that they cannot be put to any practical use. No notion could be falser, no supposition could be more baseless. The condition of realized spirituality is no nebulous and unsubstantial thing. The spiritual life can be made intensely practical in its application, indeed, properly understood, it is the best possible basis for practical existence. For we must learn to manage our thoughts rightly, because thought is the unseen guide of all our actions.

These far-off spiritual seekings may not appear to have any worth for the man in the street. This is indeed so if control of troubled nerves, peace of mind and quietness of heart, are of no worth. This is so if inner poise and outward self-mastery are of no worth. This is so if divine protection and providential aid in every kind of trouble, mysterious healing of illnesses and strange guidance in perplexity are of no worth. This is so if man lived for ever and the sickle of Death never came to cut short his days.

The cares of life constantly press in upon us for attention. Whilst a fierce activity dominates the world's attention, the wisdom which comes with mental quiet darkens and disappears. The more we give ourselves up to this unthinking materialism the more our diviner being becomes utterly hidden.

It will be the effort of these pages to show how a man, even when living under such conditions, even when hemmed in by apparently inescapable circumstances, can gain right direction for his material life, higher guidance to solve the problems of his daily living, divine protection in times of distress and spiritual healing for his bodily ailments.

I could quote many cases in this book in order to show that the technique of spiritual living proposed here is not merely an abstraction; it is a way wherein one can walk to obtain practical help in material affairs equally; it is a form of protective activity which bestows a sense of complete security deep in one's heart.

Whoever has discovered the secret path leading to his divine centre, can ever after demonstrate the fact of this discovery by the way he negotiates the inevitable obstacles, the unavoidable difficulties and the recurring distresses which enter human life from time to time. A higher life has begun for him.

Man, ignorant of self, creates his own unhappiness. The world masters him, when he was born to master the world. Life comes down with cruel feet, sooner or later, upon every man who knows few or many things but does not know himself. Even the dead do not escape. For death is but another form of life.

If man would acknowledge his divine possibilities as readily as he acknowledges his animal limitations, the millennium would come quickly. Let us not pray, then, for more power over other men, nor for greater wealth or wider fame; let us pray rather to have this crushing ignorance of our true self removed.

There are millions of men and women who are unhappy because they have never learnt this truth, who are the victims of their own deplorable ignorance. Under the polite surface of their lives they are filled with discontents, they are seething with discords, and their hearts are peaceless.

There is an ever-open door which few men deign to approach, but through which all men must one day pass.

It is the door to the real self of man, whose unseen portals must be groped for and felt after within the mysterious recesses of the human spirit. It is in those shadowed recesses that both thinking and feeling take their rise and therefore we may trace our way to the entrance along the path of guided thought or along the path of guided feeling. But once we cross the threshold and enter the inner silence, all troubling questions receive answer, all external wants become assured either of ample supply or of resigned understanding, and all menacing tribulations attract the divine strength by which they can be calmly faced. It is in this ineffable inner region that man must find his ultimate satisfaction, his final beatitude, his assured protection.

The rational basis of these things is simply explained. Man is a miniature universe in himself. His Overself constitutes the sun and his personal self plays the part of the moon. Just as the moon borrows its light from the sun, so does his personality borrow its self-consciousness and its vitality, its thinking power and feeling power, from the central luminary, the Overself. Men who live only by their personal self's wisdom and being are like men who work at night by moonlight because there is no sun. "A man who has never seen the sun," says the Spanish writer, Calderon, "cannot be blamed for thinking that no glory can exceed that of the moon." Men who live by the wisdom of the Overself can still see the contribution of the personality but place a secondary value upon it.

Something happens to the man who comes into true self-knowledge and self-ownership. He obtains a changed outlook and sees life from a new vantage ground. He looks out upon the noisy panorama of confused and troubled existence, but keeps a serene harmony within himself. The irritations which once visited him daily, fall away. The passions which once held him in their hard grip, become mellowed and are themselves caught and held by a higher force.

Success in following the Secret Path will eventually detach a man from restless desires, uncontrolled thoughts and unconsidered actions. And though the effort required may seem great, the spiritual reward will match it, for the mysterious condition betokening awareness of the Overself will one day bloom within the aspirant's soul.

In the placid moments of mental quiet we win a degree

of control over ourselves which will eventually percolate through to our daily life and permeate all our actions. This result is certain and scientific. Just as a few drops of red litmus thrown into a vessel of water will cause the latter to take on the tint of red, so *all* our external life becomes coloured with an automatic mastery over self, if we will persist in the threefold practice. Cast thy bread of time and effort upon the waters of mental quiet, and it shall be returned to thee an hundredfold.

Once you have placed yourself in the hands of the Overself within, your life will begin to flow more serenely and more sweetly. Inwardly it will be like a quiet stream, even though outwardly the storms still rage. You cannot care more for the right outcome of your affairs than the Overself cares for you. But when you handle the reins, your guidance is often ignorant and unwise; when the inner divinity handles them you will of a surety be led aright, for it is wiser than you. Give your unreserved and ungrudging surrender to it.

That which you gain in the period of mental quiet can be made available as power for living and wisdom for right action.

You will discover that the Secret Path of mental quiet will prove to be of use in every kind of situation, whether pleasurable or painful, psychological or physical. You may falter or even fail in applying this knowledge, but the Overself is infinitely patient and will be ready to assist you in its own way when you are ready to invoke its presence.

§

Little by little, imperceptibly, your daily efforts have cut a new channel within the winding convolutions of the brain, gradually rendering it easier for you to approach the sphere of influence of the Overself.

I shall now show how your work in the daily periods of mental quiet can be made to bestow a good legacy upon the rest of your day; how it can put into your hands an efficient weapon wherewith to attack problems or to defend yourself from the menace of misfortunes; and how it can come to your aid at any time to strengthen you against both temptations and trials. The method is entirely practical.

Begin by looking upon the Overself as an ever-present

Intelligence with whom you may commune, to whom you may bring your troubled heart and find peace, and under whose sheltering ægis you may dwell amply protected. Whatever your problem is, do not limit your efforts to intellectual solution only. Do not depend on the unaided reason alone. Take your difficulty into the white light of the Overself and there you will find the right guidance that will finally settle it for you.

The rule is: as often as you feel troubled, pained, perplexed, tried or tempted, first practise the placid breathing exercise for two or three minutes, then put to yourself the question:

*"Whom does this trouble?"*
*"Whom does this pain?"*
*"Whom does this perplex?"*
*"Whom does this try?"*
*"Whom does this tempt?"*

—as the case may be. After putting the appropriate silent question to yourself, pause, still your thoughts so far as you can, and repeat the "listening-in" process with which your work in mental quiet has familiarized you.

This practice opens up your consciousness to contact with the Overself, and surrounds it with the latter's protection. To switch off instantly into this quest of the spiritual self, when suddenly faced by an evil event, is to obliterate the power of this event to disturb the mind. Then, whatever necessary action will be taken will be wise and correct because it will be inspired by the Overself.

Discord has no place in the Overself. By turning inward to this Self we automatically refuse to accept the suggestions of discordant experience. When trouble arises man must refuse to accept the suggestions of despair or doubt which pour in upon his mind; instead he should calm his breathing and turn instantly in thought and inquire: "To whom has this trouble come?"

If we could reject, and reject persistently, each unpleasant, unhappy and spiritually untrue thought as it arises, we should indeed be happy mortals. The thing is perfectly practicable, but seldom by ordinary efforts of self-control; only a method such as the one presented here can accomplish such an astonishing task, for then the victory is finally gained, not by our own efforts, but by the higher power of the Overself whom we have thus invoked.

Unpleasant persons, irritating circumstances and unexpected disappointments, the undeniable effect of any of these can be nullified by making the effort to reach the divine centre of our being, and making it at once. The student must cultivate the habit of promptly turning towards the inner self when conflict with his environment threatens. If he does this faithfully, a wonderful feeling of peace and security will take possession of him, and his mind will pass, frictionless, through the occurrence.

We need to remember that our inmost selfhood is always abiding in an unalterable condition of intense peace. When troubles storm and rage around us, we should promptly repudiate undesirable reactions and attempt to centre our thought on the quest of the spiritual self. For the discovery of the latter will also be the attainment of its happy condition. The good is ever-present, but it must be sought for, felt after and recognized. No time is more suitable to take up this divine quest than when dark events and corrosive anxieties gather together for a descent upon our heads. For by a turning away of the mind into the self-quest we can demonstrate, in a manner at once striking and luminous, the mysterious power of this method. "Lift up your eyes to the heavens," admonished the old prophet, Isaiah. This turning inward of the faculty of attention necessarily weakens the strength of disharmonious and unpleasant emotions which may be attacking us. The very effort of self-finding draws us closer to the condition of sublime happiness in which the real self abides. It is a deliverance. In this way we apply the truth we have understood and make it an active factor in our lives.

The practice of this technique will infallibly obliterate fear, depression and materiality from the mind. You must refer inwards to the Overself until the habit becomes first thought, second nature and sixth sense.

The process can be explained in another way. Man, as the Overself, is desireless, is subject to no external influence, affected by no other power save the power of God. The Overself, therefore, never feels pain, is never angry and cannot be touched by depression or fear. Man, as the personal self, is filled with desires and aversions, is constantly reacting to external influences and identifies himself with them. He accepts the reactions of his body to the surroundings and to the persons it continually meets, and yields to

them as though they were really his own. He accepts the
body's registration of fear, desire, anger, repulsion, pain, and
so on. He is so unmindful of his own inner nature that he
allows the body's own ideas to rule him, and so prevents
the expression of the divine strength and powers latent in
his spiritual constitution. The moment that the mind is permitted to take on unpleasant conditions, man becomes enslaved by them and must pay the unpleasant penalty. But
if, while feeling the personal reports he persists in disre-
garding them, if he deliberately turns his face away towards
his inner centre, then the external things begin to lose their
power to affect him. In the degree that practice and habit
have developed this inward-turning faculty within himself,
will he be able to throw off malefic influences, whether they
come from other people or from his surroundings, whether
they be in the form of bodily diseases or in the form of
troubled circumstances. Nor is it surprising that such astonishing results should be obtained when we remember that
"Man was made in the image of God," and that by these
practices his true likeness gradually emerges into his consciousness.

If we open the gate of submission, of passive consciousness to discordant happenings, we have to become their
sad victims. If, however, we shut the mind's gate upon
them and yield our passivity instead to the harmonious good
in the spiritual centre of our being, we need not suffer. It
is our mental recognition of our own divinity which carries
healing on its wings and which inwardly frees us from the
malefic power of evil circumstances.

The kind of help which we may thus receive can take
various forms. Protection in times of danger is one of them.
All those who truly resign themselves to the Higher Power
receive its protective aid.

I like the frank declaration of the Red Indian chief who
wanted to attack the little Quaker meeting-house of Easton
township, in the state of New York, one bright summer
morning in the year 1775. "Indian come white man house,"
he said, pointing with his finger towards the settlement,
"Indian want kill white man, one, two, three, six, all!" and
he clutched the tomahawk at his belt with a gruesome ges-
ture. "Indian come, see white man sit in house; no gun, no
arrow, no knife; all quiet, all still, worshipping Great Spirit.

*Great Spirit inside Indian, too,"* he pointed to his breast; "then Great Spirit say: 'Indian! no kill them!'"

Healing is another form in which this aid may manifest. My friend, Dorothy Kerin, rose from a bed of death completely and instantaneously healed of advanced phthisis, diabetes and gastric ulcers. The doctors in attendance had stopped all further treatment as being hopeless. Her miraculous cure by spiritual power was the wonder of Harley Street and many medical men investigated her case, but had to admit that the healing was beyond their understanding. "My healing came direct from God," says Miss Kerin. "The New Testament is full of promises of healing, and I am confident that as soon as we are brought to open our spiritual eyes we shall see their fulfilment."

Another friend, W. T. Parish, had been told by doctors that his wife, who suffered from cancer, could not live much longer. Her left breast had already been removed by operation when the right breast was attacked. Parish took his wife away from the nursing home and began to treat her himself, by the methods and power of the spirit. In nine months she was well again. Her case offers a clear and perfect demonstration of the power of the spirit over the body, a significant pointer toward the cure of one of modernity's most dread diseases by the application of antiquity's most sublime therapeutic remedy, divine healing power.

The life-force of the Overself flows continuously into every electron in every atom which goes to form the body. It is the Overself which really gives life to our bodies and sustains them. Without its invisible presence our bodies would instantly collapse dead, pieces of inert matter. The machinery of the body could not revolve without its unseen spiritual belts. And it is the Overself which can likewise repair and heal those bodies.

The power of the Overself is with you here and now; nothing can shut you out of its operation except your own wilful neglect, your own supine doubt. Follow the Secret Path and appropriate that which is already yours.

Nevertheless, man cannot dictate to the Creative Intelligence which rules the world and informs his life, as to the exact form in which he shall receive aid, nor can he always demand satisfaction of his personal needs irrespective of higher considerations. In the last analysis man is a pensioner on the universal bounty.

He cannot always govern circumstances, but he can govern his response to them. If spiritual realization may not always remove the shadows of poverty, illness or misfortune from his path, it will bestow on him the courage to battle with poverty, the patience to endure sickness and the wisdom with which to face misfortune.

The man who enters increasingly into this awareness of his deeper self will feel less inclined to importune the powers-that-be for his success, his material needs and his social wants. Instead, he will feel the protective power of this self, and if he petitions it at all, it will be for more wisdom, more strength and more love. Having these things, he knows that he can safely leave the rest to the divinity within, which will then unfailingly meet his *true* needs at the appointed hour.

It is good to know that we can live all the more securely if we make and keep open some line of retreat into the Overself. We can walk this old earth of ours all the more safely if we take ticket for the stars now and then.

Let us look for the Overself through the mist of unsought tears, through the sunshine of gratified desires, and let us not forget what we really are.

A man is but mediocre until he learns to trust this higher power, the real self, until he makes it a living factor in his outlook and looks always within for its leading.

Believe in the self you know and you are at once limited, believe in the greater self which you really are and you may go on and on to achievement. BE what you have it within you to be.

In your serenest exaltations you will realize this profound truth, *that you have never really parted from God!*

## CHAPTER XII

### THE EPILOGUE

YES—you have never really parted from the Divine Power which controls the universe, governs the life of man, and is the unseen basis of all existence. Is this not a helpful thought at a time like the present, when we live in a period of frank disbelief and cynical materialism, results of the fact that the human race has been put on its Golgotha since 1914. Browning's rosy-tinted sentence: "God's in His heaven, all's well with the world," is read through black spectacles. We are wearily dubious about the existence of God and of His heaven, while the present aspect of the world seems to throw the lie in Browning's face.

The serious literature of the last few years has become a literature of despair. The men who think and the men who write for something more than the mere entertainment of others, have begun to see how significant are the challenging issues which time is rapidly bringing to a crisis. They see that the auroral glow which hung around the hopes of the entire world when the war ended has faded and that we are left with a bewildering fog. They have been forced, despite themselves, to become reluctant harbingers of doom. They have to-day become croaking Cassandras prophetically warning humanity of coming woes. We leave the last page of their writings with a feeling of chill and an impression of deep pessimism.

Who that watches the social and political edifices around us crumbling or crashing to the ground can doubt that he is watching the close of a great historical epoch? To-day the tale of history has become the drama of the unexpected; we wait for the next fresh surprise each morning. The long continued Manchu Dynasty has made its exit from Peking, and the country which created the Gold Standard has gone off it. The only certain thing to-day is uncertainty. The caravan of life once wound through the ages like an endless procession, but nowadays it dashes along on high-speed engines.

Mankind to-day is both hungry and haunted; hungry for a better and brighter age yet haunted by the heavy shadows of the past. The world seems willing to try every way but the right way. Troubled by the prospects of another war, perturbed by the chaotic political conditions of every continent, it rushes hither and thither in its quest of the perfectly efficient formula which will solve its economic and political problems. But the one perfect formula, the one infallible formula, though within its grasp, is beyond its vision. And that is—the Golden Rule! "Do unto others what you would have them do to you."

The crying need of the world to-day is not for a change of head but a change of heart. There is no lack of ideas among us—rather the reverse—but there is a lack of goodwill. The feeling of goodwill will be the best insurance of universal peace.

Who can gaze upon the spectacle of modern Europe and not remember the warning utterance of the Prophet of Nazareth, an utterance which is written in fiery letters across the pages of history. Who can forget those terrible words of Jesus, when he stood upon Mount Olivet and indicted the chief city of the Jews:

"O Jerusalem, Jerusalem, thou that killest the prophets and stonest them which are sent unto thee, how often would I have gathered thy children together, even as a hen gathereth her chickens under her wings, and ye would not."

§

We must stand for awhile, however, as did Clio, the historical Muse, in ancient times, with pen suspended, and not rush to set down judgment upon our age. For there is a plan behind the events which pattern the modern world's life, and unless man has learnt to discern this plan he cannot judge aright.

*The powers which guide the universe, which guard mankind and watch over the world, will speak to this century in tones much more forceful than mine and demonstrate their existence through events far more startling than the publication of a mere book.* Because we gaze around and see the chaos that broods upon us, the foolish fear that God is dead or absent and that we are lost. Because no hand stretches forth out of the Great Unknown to save mankind from its self-earned sorrows, they imagine that there *is* no hand to help us. God could, if He willed, heal all the sorrows of this planet in an instant of time. But that would be to transform us into automatons, to turn us into machine-made angels. Man, if he is to grow Godlike, must do so of his own free will. And the guarantee that he will do so is the presence of a divine spark within himself. There are true voices in the heart—the voices of Hope and Good-will, and these shall once more be heard.

For the divine instinct in man is ineradicable; it may be covered up for a time, but it must one day well forth again.

It is trite, but true, that man's extremity is God's opportunity. What applies to an individual applies equally to a nation, which is but a collection of individuals, and equally to the whole world, which is but a collection of nations. Social distress, economic anxiety, political chaos—all these are, after all, but the physical consequences of the lack of spirituality in the world. The world's extremity will prove to be God's opportunity and the history of the twentieth century will fully evidence this fact.

The Biblical story of the prodigal son has a world meaning as well as a personal one, and when the peoples are tired of their endless self-caused troubles, beaten by their Frankenstein monsters of scientifically-waged wars that are mass massacres and disastrous economic plights that reveal their lack of good-will, they will turn their faces homewards and set out on the journey back to a better life. And their Father, knowing this, will go towards them and meet them, kiss and comfort them and reveal his unbroken love for them.

Meanwhile, the supreme question still faces man: dost know thyself? In this troubled and fateful time, the wise man will seek an unshakable foothold, whereon he can rest while the world whirls madly around him. Such a foothold cannot be found in any external place; it is only to be discovered in the secret depths of the heart. There, in the mysterious recesses of our own being, it exists, giving man a deeper strength and higher wisdom. The man who is wise with the wisdom of the Overself and strong in its strength has other business in hand than passively waiting for new Armageddons or planetary cataclysms. There is no fear for the morrow for him who lives in this absolute trust, just as the sparrows have no fear for their morrows.

He knows that the night will pass, and dawn, silent and irresistible, will roll back the world's darkness and once more flood it with light. When the truth about the hidden side of the universe and of man is once more unveiled, demonstrated so far as it can be in a scientific and rational manner, the new scientific findings will stagger the most powerful intellects. We shall then build a pillar of higher wisdom which shall rise up into a new and finer age, and we shall testify anew to those eternal spiritual truths which no advance of science, no progress of civilization, no lapse in human character, can ever render obsolete.

Meanwhile, each of us who practises this secret inner way can become a disseminator of the true light, can change himself and thus become fit to change others. It is to such men, inspired selfless instruments, ready to work in the higher service of mankind, that we must look for the liberation of the world from its legacy of spiritual ignorance and material sufferings.

Let us submit to the grandeur of the imperishable Overself; even when we cannot understand it or grasp its Himalayan attitude, let us nevertheless yield mind and heart and body to its august behests. Thus we enter into undying life and gather the immortal fruits of truth, wisdom, peace and power.

Let us offer ourselves to the powers-that-be that they may use us to serve mankind nobly in the sphere that has fallen to us, however circumscribed it be; let us silently give ourselves for the inner welfare of others, even as Christ has given Himself for the welfare of this shadowed planet; let us be true to the unseen purpose which the gods hold eternally before mankind. For there is everywhere present the divine life; shall we betray it by denying its deathless existence, or shame it by despising its sublime monitions?

**MAY PEACE BE WITH YOU**